Give Us a Word

A Collection of Sermons for Christians Today

John L. Blackburn

CLAY BRIDGES
PRESS

Give Us a Word
A Collection of Sermons for Christians Today

Published by Clay Bridges in Houston, TX
www.claybridgespress.com

ISBN 978-1-953300-81-2 (paperback)
ISBN 978-1-953300-82-9 (hardback)
ISBN 978-1-953300-80-5 (ebook)

Special Sales: Most Clay Bridges titles are available in special quantity discounts. Custom imprinting or excerpting can also be done to fit special needs. For standard bulk orders, go to www.claybridgesbulk.com. For specialty press or large orders, contact Clay Bridges at info@claybridgespress.com.

Table of Contents

Introduction	1
Pursue Peace	5
Grasping for Crumbs	11
Children of the Light	15
Blessed Are Those	19
Thomas the Doubter	25
Already, Not Yet	31
Mary and Martha	37
Money Bins and Silos	43
Finding the Lost Sheep	49
Remembering the Human Element	53
The Kingdom of God	59
Do Not Be Afraid	63
The Light of the World	69
A Lifelong Apprenticeship	75
The Logic of the Cross	83
Choose Life	89
Trapped in the Dark	95
The Unknown God	101
Can These Bones Live?	109
Who Better to Serve Than Christ?	115
Acknowledgments	121

Introduction

In the early centuries of Christianity, one of the curious modes of devoting your life to Christ was to become a hermit and live alone in seclusion. There were many of these so-called Desert Fathers, and some became known as great teachers. As time passed, people traveled out of the cities to go and spend time with these hermits and early monks. These holy and devout men and women (yes, there were also women) sometimes spent days or weeks in complete silence until they were ready to teach. Usually when travelers approached one of these fathers for teaching or spiritual guidance, they said, "Abba! Give me a word!"

This book is a collection of sermons preached over the course of about three years. Some of them were preached in church settings on Sunday mornings, and others were preached in seminary chapels, either for one of the Daily Offices such as Evening Prayer or for a Sunday morning Eucharist Liturgy. Some are a little academic, while others were written and preached with a specific congregation or parishioners in mind.

Preaching a sermon to the faithful week after week is a challenging task for any minister of the gospel. There is a line that must be toed each week, but the line is complicated. First, there is your congregation's knowledge. You can't preach over the top of their heads, and you can't preach beneath them—you have to find that middle ground. Second, you can't preach the same sermon each week or even the same sermon each year around certain themes such as the resurrection or the mystery of the incarnation. You have to be fresh, timely, and relevant to your location and the people you are gazing at from the pulpit. Third, sermons must be lively and imaginative; they must possess both a spirit of the divine and the fullness of humanity. And finally, sermons and homilies must be preached out of love—love of God, love of your congregation, and love of the church. That can be the most challenging task for many preachers. My hope is that I fulfill each of these tasks weekly or sometimes several times a week.

Within these pages are some of the sermons I either truly enjoyed and relished the opportunity to write and preach or found the response of the hearers more encouraging than I had expected. Some of these were wrestling matches to write; others came quickly in a matter of a few hours. But as I pray to myself each time before I speak, may the words I speak with my lips be transformed by God's grace to what the listeners need to hear with their ears.

I mentioned that sermons must be timely, must be fresh, and must be relevant to the congregation. With that in mind, the editors and I were faced with a choice about a few of the sermons in this book and one in particular. Do we include sermons that reference the coronavirus pandemic, or do we rewrite those portions? Do we include references to what are now historical events, perhaps two or three years old by the time this book is published? And do we remove the hint of location in some of the sermons?

Here is what we ultimately decided. First, we would remove hints about locations. While it is important to know your congregation and your city, there is a universal appeal to the gospel, so we excised all references to particular churches and cities where I preached these sermons. Second, we do learn from history, diaries, journals, and church newsletters, which are all good historical records of events that have happened. In a way, so too are the recorded sermons of the church. How was the church dealing with the issues of the day? What gave them hope? What word was important for them to hear? Third, near the end of this collection, you will see a sermon based on Ezekiel's vision of the valley of the dry bones. I preached it during Lent 2020 at the beginning of the global COVID-19 pandemic. I tried to reimagine the sermon and put a different spin on it, but I couldn't. It was the first time I had ever preached to a nearly empty church with only a priest and a cantor present. I spoke into a camera, trying to imagine what the people watching were feeling—their concerns, their worries, and their grief at not being with us as the body of Christ. Memories of that event still bring tears to my eyes. So I decided to leave that sermon intact and not edit it or strike it from this collection. I hope it is a reminder to us all of both a time when so much seemed lost and what a post-pandemic world might look like.

In my tradition, the Episcopal Church and the wider Anglican Communion have a prescribed set of readings known as the Lectionary. In it are readings assigned for every day of the year and for different services that may be held. Generally, there are one or two readings and several psalms for Morning or Evening Prayer (sometimes known as Matins or Evensong if a choir sings portions of the service) or three readings and a portion of a psalm on Sundays and feast days. Each of the sermons in this collection is based on one or two Lectionary readings for a particular day. To help the reader, the Scripture reference is at the top of each sermon. Because the congregation heard these readings just before the sermon, I encourage you to read them before reading the actual sermon. And read carefully! Read slowly! Even if you are reading this book on the go with the advancement and wonders of technology, it is very easy to find the Scripture references on our mobile phones, tablets, laptops, and various Bible apps.

Finally, my fervent wish and desire is that you find this book helpful, enlightening, and engaging. My prayer is that God's grace will take these words of mine in this little collection and transform them into something useful to you.

Soli Deo Gloria,

John L. Blackburn
March 9, 2021

The Feast of Saint Gregory, Bishop of Nyssa, cir. 394

Pursue Peace

Hebrews 12:12–29

*In the Name of the Father, and of the Son, and of the
Holy Spirit. Amen.*

I belong to a group that is not a chartered organization and doesn't meet at any official time. Rather, this group is 13 people who just so happen to enjoy each other's company. Many of us found one another around the same time, and for about four years now we've been as thick as thieves. What we do is simple. We eat together (usually Thursdays at lunch), we travel together, we hunt together, and we celebrate each other's birthdays together. Once, we even took a member's wife out for her first wedding anniversary because her husband had to travel for work and couldn't be in town for their anniversary. We watch sporting events together, and we sometimes just enjoy being with one another without any agenda. Sometimes it is two or three of us who meet; other times all 13 come together. We are just a group.

And we like each other's company—most of the time. That's the strain in relationships. Usually, everything is hunky-dory and we all cooperate, get along, have a great time, and make great memories—most of the time.

But on occasion, something happens. Either someone interrupts someone else too many times or someone gets upset about not getting enough attention. At times, we call someone out for doing something they know they ought not to do, and that causes a small fracas. And sometimes, for reasons unknown to anyone in the group, someone is just put out. Recently, two of our members had such a serious disagreement that one threatened to leave the group, and the other actually did.

Our group is like other groups, and there can be internal problems just like many organizations—football and soccer teams, close-knit business partners, people who work with a charity, political parties (just watch the news and you can see), and the church. Yes, the church is perhaps chief among them. This institution is supposed to be a beacon to the world, a model of how to live together in community, an engine room that provides power and encouragement for doing the work of Christ in the world—but yes, this group can also be beset by controversies. One of our hymns even tells us the church is not immune: "by schisms rent asunder, by heresies distressed" and "mid toil and tribulation, and tumult of her war, she waits the consummation of peace forevermore."[1]

Our passage from Hebrews gives us this pointed command: pursue peace with everyone. Pursue it. Don't wait idly by for it. Pursue. Chase. Hunt. Track it. Go after it with every fiber

---

1. Samuel John Stone, "The Church's One Foundation," *The Hymnal 1982* (New York: The Church Hymnal Corporation, 1985), Hymn 525.

of your being. Pursuing peace isn't quite like the phrase we often hear from Miss America contenders—"and I hope to work for world peace." Rather, it is a gut-wrenching, dirty process that may mean we end up being hurt even a little more when we offer an apology and it is rejected, when our spouse who hurt us refuses to acknowledge any blame for their part of the crisis, or when the elderly lady in the pew in front of us says something hurtful about the ministry we do. Look at the struggles of many of our saints and holy people such as Archbishop Oscar Romero, Martin Luther King Jr., Dietrich Bonhoeffer, Archbishop Desmond Tutu, and the list goes on and on. Pursue peace.

Why?

We have answers throughout Scripture as to why. Perhaps the most familiar is Peter's question that asks how often to forgive. Seven times? I can imagine him saying it with glee knowing he may have finally answered a question correctly. Surely seven times is enough. But Jesus, surely somewhat chuckling to himself, said something like this: "No, Peter . . . no, no, no. Let's try 77 times."[2]

In the Gospel of Matthew, Jesus warns about division in the church and how to reestablish peace between two believers.[3] Even earlier, still in Matthew, Jesus warns us that it may be more important to get ourselves right with each other first before offering ourselves and our gifts to God. "So when you are offering your gift at the altar, if you remember that your brother or sister has something against you, leave your gift there before

---

2. See Matt. 18:21–22.
3. See Matt. 18:15–20.

the altar and go; first be reconciled to your brother or sister, and then come and offer your gift" (Matt. 5:23–24). Be reconciled. Pursue peace.

And what happens if we don't? Our reading says that bitterness will take root, there will be trouble, and "through it many become defiled" (Heb. 12:15). How is that so?

Think about our own friends who, for whatever reason, fight and disagree to a point where they ask us to take sides. Or consider the couple getting a divorce who attempt to rally supporters to their side. Or even look at the churches that split into two factions, making it quite clear there is no room for both, not only in the church but also at the communion rail. We have seen this behavior throughout the history of the church—the Great Schism and the Reformation come to mind. But there are also the local church members who get angry at one another about anything and everything, even something as small as the carpet not being the right color.

Esau, who sold his birthright to Jacob, is called an immoral and godless man. It is not because Esau was hungry and sold his birthright but because Esau was hungry *in the moment*. Esau let a fleeting feeling of displeasure and discomfort overtake his senses, and he sold what was his right as the firstborn. Esau let one poor decision control his fate, his inheritance, and summarily his destiny. Because of his empty stomach, Esau was left without much, and then because of Jacob's cunning, Esau was left with even less. The author of Hebrews says that "when he [Esau] wanted to inherit the blessing, he was rejected, for he found no chance to repent, even though he sought the blessing with tears" (Heb. 12:17). How often do we let one moment of bad judgment, one moment of indiscretion, dictate and ruin our lives and our relationships?

Let us not be like Esau and wait until it is too late. Rather, let us confront head-on those instances where we are the people who disrupt the peace of our friends and families, the peace of our communities, and the peace of the church. How much better it is to work at putting relationships back together and mending friendships, both as individuals and as members of the church! Let us not be like Esau who let one bad decision in one particular circumstance cause his relationship with his brother, his father, and his mother to deteriorate.

When one person left my group of 13, it was a difficult situation. The member who left formed a separate group, leaving out the member who offended him, which damaged the relationships even more. A few people chose sides, and the member who stayed became rather angry with the ones who chose to side with the member who left. For about a month it was rather nasty. Alliances were drawn, some people avoided lunch if certain people were going, Christmas parties were in chaos, and some people felt unwelcome at certain events. And then, when neither offending member was around, the group talked equally badly about both of them!

But one day, the member who had stayed in the group sent a message to the member who had left, and in that message was an olive branch: "Hey—this whole thing is rather stupid. I'm sorry I hurt your feelings. When you get back into town, why don't we get together and sort out our differences."

Within minutes, the former member replied, "Yep, this is stupid. I'll be back in about two weeks."

Moments later, the second group thread had a message that it was wrong and hurtful to start a second thread, and it was dissolved. The group began to unify again. Yes, there was healing that needed to happen, and honestly, there probably still is. Two people decided to pursue peace. Two people decided to dig up a bitter root and burn it. Two people decided their differences were not worth defiling a group of friends with whom they had so much in common.

Pursue peace with everyone, and pursue holiness, without which no one will see the Lord.

Grasping for Crumbs

Mark 7:24–37

In the Name of the Father, and of the Son, and of the Holy Spirit. Amen.

If the Gospel of Mark has a proverbial elephant in the room, it is probably the passage where Jesus, our loving and compassionate Savior, appears to take a woman to task who is part of the "other." He calls her a dog but then ends up healing her daughter who is possessed by a demon. What's going on here?

First, Jesus has traveled to Tyre, a Gentile-dominated area just north of Israel. Wanting to remain secluded and perhaps even rest for a few moments, Jesus goes into a house. In traditional Marcian form, the woman *immediately* hears about Jesus's arrival and goes to him with a supplication on bended knee to cast the demon out of her daughter. Jesus shocks and stuns us with his retort. Let's break this down.

It was common in that time period and region for different groups to insult each person who wasn't a member of their cultural and national group. Jesus's calling the woman a dog could almost be akin to calling her the family pet, the pet that stays under the table waiting for a handout from someone. Jesus is in the process of inaugurating the Kingdom of God, and his view is that the Kingdom must come from and be presented by the Jewish world first. Géza Vermes put it this way: "In these unequivocal utterances, Jesus is presented as the champion of absolute Jewish exclusivism."[1] Jesus is harkening back to his view of Isaiah and the restoration of both the nation of Israel and this inauguration of the Kingdom of God. For example, in the First Servant Song, Isaiah writes, "I have given you as a covenant to the people, a light to the nations, to open the eyes that are blind, to bring out the prisoners from the dungeon" (Isa. 42:6–7). The *Nunc dimittis*[2] further reminds us of Simeon's prophecy that echoes the same refrain: "A light to lighten the Gentiles, and the glory of thy people Israel" (Luke 2:32 KJV).

If you notice carefully, Jesus doesn't say, "No, not for you, you Gentile dog!" He instead says that the children of Israel needed to be fed first. Jesus is making clear that the gospel he is proclaiming is for the Jewish people first so the nation of Israel can be the light to the nations it was meant to be from the very foundation of the world.

But what about this woman? We can use adjectives and phrases to describe her such as tenacious, turning the tables on

1. Géza Vermes, *The Authentic Gospel of Jesus* (London: Penguin Books, 2003), 377.
2. Also called the Song of Simeon.

Jesus, desperate, full of faith, putting Jesus in his place—the list could go on. I prefer to describe our friend here as someone with insistent, compelling faith, someone who is a prime model and exemplar for all of us.

How often do we give up on our own prayer life and flippantly say to ourselves, "Whatever God wants, he will just do. It doesn't matter if I ask and pray; it doesn't matter if I ask my friends to pray. Nothing is ever answered. Perhaps God doesn't even care!" This is where we are dreadfully and dangerously wrong.

Let us ponder two incidents in Genesis that show the nature of God and our requests. The first is Abraham bargaining with God over the destruction of Sodom and Gomorrah. Abraham plays the role of a reserve auctioneer: "God, what about 50, 45, 40, 30, surely 20—no, how about 10? 10! Done deal!" Abraham's tenacity and faith about who he knew God to be allowed him the courage to continue to ask and persuade the Lord God.

The second episode is Jacob striving with God all night until the Divine forces Jacob's hip out of its socket and renames him. His new name is Israel—he who has striven with God and with humans and has prevailed.

Israel—a person who strives with God.

Israel—a nation that strove with God.

Perhaps the Syrophoenican woman in our passage in Mark is a symbol of the New Israel—the Gentile nations who have seen the light of Israel—and the crumbs they've gathered under the table give them all a taste of the glory of God. Perhaps she is a symbol of who we are and what we are, people always yearning for crumbs from Jesus because those crumbs are just enough to satisfy us.

One of the prayers of the church that we sometimes say during the Eucharistic Prayers recalls this moment and grappling with Jesus: "We are not worthy so much as to gather up the crumbs under thy Table. But thou are the same Lord whose property is *always* to have mercy" (emphasis added).[3]

She asked, and it was given unto her.

She sought, she strove, she argued, and she received her request.

May we have the courage, tenacity, and fortitude to be portrayers of insistent and compelling faith in our own day.

---

3. "The Prayer of Humble Access," *Book of Common Prayer* (New York: The Church Hymnal Corporation, 1979), 337.

Children of the
Light

1 John 3:1–8

In the Name of the Father, and of the Son, and of the
Holy Spirit. Amen.

Every year on February 2nd, Christians around the world
celebrate Candlemas, or the Presentation of Our Lord
Jesus Christ in the Temple. The Gospel of Luke records
this event: "When the time came for their purification according
to the law of Moses, they brought him [Jesus] up to Jerusalem to
present him to the Lord (as it is written in the law of the Lord,
'Every firstborn male shall be designated as holy to the Lord')"
(Luke 2:22–23). Following the Law of Moses, Joseph and Mary
traveled to the Temple and followed the rites and ceremonies
for Mary's purification, since giving birth rendered her ritually
unclean. They made a sacrifice and gave their firstborn child as

a dedication to the Lord. That's the first part of the story for the Candlemas feast.

The second part of the story stems from a little later in the chapter. We meet an older man, Simeon, who extols God for keeping a promise that he would see "a light for revelation to the Gentiles" (Luke 2:32). It is this little portion of the *Nunc dimittis* that serves as a catalyst for the celebration of Candlemas. Not all that long ago, the tradition of Christians was to bring candles, sometimes even their year's supply, to the church on this day to be blessed by the priest. Hopefully, the candles helped serve as a reminder to everyone of that Light that was indeed a revelation to the Gentiles and continues to do so.

Jesus refers to himself in the Gospel of John as light: "I am the light of the world. Whoever follows me will never walk in darkness but will have the light of life" (John 8:12). It is this light that our epistle writer grasps in the early verses of 1 John: "God is light and in him there is no darkness at all. If we say that we have fellowship with him while we are walking in darkness, we lie and do not do what it true" (1 John 1:5–6).

Our passage for this chapter draws upon these ideas of being children of God and children of light. And being children of light, we should do what is right, what is wholesome, and what is pure. We should live righteously; we should live lives that are purified. If we do not, we sin, live in sin, and act as if we are children of the devil.

If a room was dark and you lit a candle, that candle would illumine everything in the room. But if you took a filter of some sort and blocked part of that delicate light, you would see less clearly. Sin can be like that in our lives. Some sins we regard as little sins—being curt with our friends or family, being jealous of others' achievements, lying to someone to avoid a hard answer.

Other sins we seem to regard as more serious—murder, adultery, some sort of social irresponsibility. Even if we view sin on a sliding scale, what type of light are we exuding when we, in fact, do sin, even little sins? Just like the candle that gets dimmer and fainter if you cover it or move it away, our reflection, our illumination as children of the light becomes fainter and harder to recognize. It becomes harder for others to see the light in us and perhaps harder still for us to recognize it in ourselves.

We all sin. Each of us falls short every day—we miss the mark. But John's argument in this reading is preceded by great hope and good news: "If anyone does sin, we have an advocate with the Father, Jesus Christ the righteous, and he is the atoning sacrifice for our sins, and not for ours only but also for the sins of the whole world" (1 John 2:1–2).

Consider this verse: "All who have this hope in him purify themselves" (1 John 3:3). Just as Mary went to the Temple for her purification, and just as Jesus is the atoning sacrifice and our advocate, so may all of us also strive to purify our own lives. Light and purity go hand in hand. One of our ancient prayers reminds of this: "O gracious Light, pure brightness of the everliving Father in heaven."[1] There is no such thing as dirty light—only light that may have to struggle through a dirty filter.

When you see candles that are lit, use that as a reminder of this Feast of Candlemas and its significance. But see them also as a reminder to live a life undimmed and unstained by sin.

---

1. "The Phos hilaron," *Book of Common Prayer*, 1979, 118.

Blessed Are Those

Luke 6:17–26

In the Name of the Father, and of the Son, and of the Holy Spirit. Amen.

One of the classic elements in police investigative work is to gather evidence and statements from as many eyewitnesses as possible. By collecting information from a variety of sources, detectives and others can begin to paint a picture of what happened at the scene of a crime. However, there is always one problem that looms large as they go about their work. What happens when you have two, three, or more people whose memories of crucial details differ? Was the suspect wearing a hat? What color was his shirt? How much do you think he weighed, or how tall was he? What model car did he get away in? People who have seen the same event often remember things in slightly different ways.

Much of the same can be said about our passage from the Gospel of Luke. At first hearing, we all might sit back and say to ourselves, "Oh yes! Those wonderful beatitudes of Jesus. How lovely they are!" As we settle into the first bit of the passage, however, we realize that Luke's account is somewhat different from Matthew's, and by the end we are all rather disturbed because Jesus is actually pronouncing curses on a few people—perhaps even you and me. Matthew and Luke have seen the same event yet have walked away with rather different opinions of what Jesus said. Let's take a quick examination of Matthew's account.

First, Matthew has Jesus preaching to a great multitude on a mountain while he is sitting down (a common posture for rabbis and teachers in the ancient world). With images that would have been recognizable to a Jewish audience, Matthew almost portrays Jesus as a Moses-like figure bringing down the Law from Mount Sinai to the multitudes. Second, the passages that are paralleled in Matthew and Luke both begin with "blessed are," but from there they quickly diverge and tend to not agree with what or who the blessed are. For example, Matthew says, "Blessed are the poor in spirit, for theirs is the kingdom of heaven" (Matt. 5:3). A few verses later he writes, "Blessed are those who hunger and thirst for righteousness, for they will be filled" (Matt. 5:6). Third, as you can draw from these two examples, Matthew's recording of the Beatitudes are wonderful examples of spiritualized and intangible needs and desires.

Luke tells a slightly different story. Instead of sitting on a hillside, Jesus has come down from the mountain and is on a plain, teaching not the whole crowd but only his disciples. The next major point of difference is Luke's record of the Beatitudes. The poor are not simply poor in spirit; they are poor. The hungry are not just hungry for justice; they are hungry for bread. And to drive the point home a little further, Jesus is not talking about someone we may happen to run across. He is talking about *you* who are poor, *you* who are hungry, *you* who are weeping. Instead of discussing a highly spiritualized state, Jesus is talking about social and economic conditions, about physical conditions and states of being that all of us know about and some of us may have even experienced.

Perhaps the most biting part of the Sermon on the Plain is the end of our reading in Luke. Jesus pronounces a series of woes in direct contrast to the blessings he just pronounced. Woe to you who are rich. Woe to you who are satisfied and full. Woe to you who laugh. What is going on here? Why is Jesus condemning what many of us seek? We desire to be rich and satisfied. We do not want to worry about where the next meal is coming from, and we want to be filled with joy and laughter. Jesus is talking to his disciples, and by extension of discipleship, he is talking to us today as well.

As disciples, we are called to go where Jesus goes, to minister to the people Jesus sought out. The loving embrace of Jesus includes everyone—rich, poor, hungry, satisfied—and there is not anyone outside of that saving embrace. However, when we are rich, the question arises about who or what we put our trust in. When we eat three rather generous square meals a day, how do we share the excess of our bounty? When we laugh at the expense of others and their misery, where is the love of God we should be sharing? Jesus never condemns wealth. What Jesus does condemn, what the prophets centuries before him condemned, and what Mary even juxtaposes in the Magnificat is trusting in wealth for our security and safety. When we trust in something so earthly as money, when do we trust in God? "No slave can serve two masters" (Luke 16:13). When we eat until we are full and do not share even a morsel of bread with those in need, how do we then live as disciples? "He has filled the hungry with good things, and sent the rich away empty" (Luke 1:53). When we laugh at the peril of others around us, how can we then show the love of God to others who so desperately need it? "When the Lord saw her, he had compassion for her" (Luke 7:13). The poor aren't blessed because they are poor; the poor are blessed because of who they trust.

Rowan Williams, the former Archbishop of Canterbury, wrote two tiny books. The first book, *Being Christian*, details what makes us Christians—baptism, Bible, Eucharist, and prayer. The second book, *Being Disciples*, is a more challenging read. Yes, we should all be Christians, but we should also be good disciples. The Sermon on the Plain is a clarion call to us as Christians to look at the world around us, to see the needs that exist, and to look at the suffering and anguish of others. It is not until we leave the security of status and plenty that we can go where Jesus calls us to go. Williams says it this way: "We are in the middle of two things that seem quite contradictory: In the middle of the heart of God, the ecstatic joy of the Father, the Son and the Holy Spirit; and in the middle of a world of threat, suffering, sin and pain. And because Jesus has taken his stand right in the middle of those two realities, that is where we take ours."[1]

When we are able to gaze on the world around us, when we see all the work yet to be done, and when we answer that calling and urging from God, perhaps the most difficult thing to accept is what people will say. What will the neighbors think? What is Bill at the coffee shop going to say? "Blessed are you when people hate you, and when they exclude you, revile you, and defame you on account of the Son of Man" (Luke 6:22). The call of being

---

1. Rowan Williams, *Being Christian: Baptism, Bible, Eucharist, Prayer*. (Grand Rapids, MI: Eerdmans, 2014), 7, Google Books.

Christians—of being disciples—is a hard burden to bear. "If any want to become my followers, let them deny themselves and take up their cross daily and *follow me*" (emphasis added) (Luke 9:23). Disciples abide with their Master. They follow their Teacher. They go and do the things their Teacher does. Our call today, just as it was on the plain, is to focus our love, our trust, and our devotion on Jesus without the distraction of wealth, bounty, and status. When we follow our Master and our Friend, all the injustices of this world will vanish. And when we learn to see the poor, the hungry, the sorrowful, and the outcast as people Jesus loves, we learn a little more about what it means to be good disciples. Then our "reward is great in heaven" (Luke 6:23).

Thomas the Doubter

John 20:19–31

In the Name of the Father, and of the Son, and of the
Holy Spirit. Amen.

Poor Thomas! Poor, poor Thomas! If ever there was a disciple who ended up with a questionable or ruined reputation, it was Thomas. We have even given him a dubious nickname, Doubting Thomas. Thomas was a disciple, an apostle, and a member of Jesus's close circle of friends. Later, after the events of the Gospel of John and the Day of Pentecost, Christian history records him as being one of the most successful missionaries of the first century. He is credited with planting churches in the East and traveling as far as current-day India, Pakistan, Afghanistan, and perhaps even the borderlands of China. So this begs the question: why are we so unfair to Thomas?

Let's take a little trip through the Gospels so we might understand what Thomas may have been thinking. A few chapters earlier in John's Gospel, Lazarus, who was undoubtedly known to the disciples, is very ill and later dies. When Jesus announces they are going to return to Judea, the disciples rebuke Jesus and say, "Rabbi, the Jews were just now trying to stone you, and are you going there again?" (John 11:8). But guess who is the first to commit when we hear a few verses later, "Let us also go, that we may die with him" (John 11:16). It's Thomas! To me, it sounds more like a true sign of courage and faith to stand up to his friends while he maintains an unpopular position, even when that position is standing alongside Jesus.

Moving forward in the Gospel of John, Jesus begins his farewell discourse, a soliloquy of things to remember that he tells his disciples just hours before his crucifixion. Jesus is telling them not to be troubled, that he is going to prepare a place for his disciples, and "You know the way to the place where I am going" (John 14:4). Thomas, ever the practical one, utterly misunderstands and says with a hint of desperation, "Lord, we do not know where you are going. How can we know the way?" (John 14:5). Thomas certainly isn't doubting here. He's looking for answers to questions he has. Jesus's answer to Thomas is perhaps one of the most cherished lines in all Scripture. "I am the way, and the truth, and the life" (John 14:6).

This brings us to our passage of Scripture. Jesus is resurrected. He has appeared to Mary Magdalene, and as the Gospel of John opens, we learn it is evening of that same Easter Day. The disciples are gathered together behind a locked door, and they are afraid—that is, all of them except Thomas. Where's Thomas? Has he abandoned the cause? Is he out looking for answers to the deep, hard questions he was asking because of what just happened?

Showing the courage he exhibited earlier, perhaps Thomas is already starting a new mission based on Jesus's teachings. We will never know. All we do know is that the disciples eventually make contact with Thomas before the week is finished. They tell him what they have seen, and he makes an argument for empirical verification: "Unless I see the mark of the nails in his hands, and put my finger in the mark of the nails and my hand in his side, I will not believe" (John 20:25).

Thomas the courageous. Thomas the practical. But here is where we get into trouble. We leap to judgment and false conclusions, and Thomas gets labeled "the Doubter." But let's think about this for a moment. Jesus had appeared to everyone *but* Thomas. He had appeared to Mary Magdalene. He had been with the rest of the disciples. Did Thomas make this statement out of frustration? Did he regard himself as a second-class disciple? Why hadn't he been given an invitation to the resurrection party?

"Unless I see. . . ." Mary had *seen*. The disciples had *seen*. Earlier in the same chapter, John the beloved disciple had run to the tomb with Peter, and he had *seen*. The tomb was empty, and he believed. Thomas was asking for what everyone else around him had already experienced—seeing Jesus in a resurrected body, seeing Jesus alive again. He wanted to be able to rejoice about what *he* was seeing!

How often are we like Thomas? I know I doubt things every day, and it isn't always about doubting God. I know I sometimes question things I know are true, but for reasons that sometimes cannot be explained, I call those truths into question. For instance, do we doubt love and friendship for those closest to us? Perhaps we self-doubt—am I really qualified or capable of performing the task set before me? Maybe it's depressing doubt, the kind you get by watching everyone around you succeed or get the job promotion you want, and you wonder if your luck is just bad. And sometimes, even when we pray, read our Bibles, and go to church week after week, we are like Thomas and wonder why we aren't seeing the same things everyone else seems to see.

And so in this passage, it is a week later. Thomas is with the other disciples, and Jesus comes. Does Jesus reprimand Thomas for his doubt? No. Does he tell Thomas to get out of his sight because he is unworthy for his lack of faith? No. Does he tell Thomas that before he can enjoy the benefits of being a Christian he has to go to remedial classes led by Peter who had denied Jesus three times a little over a week ago? No! He welcomes Thomas and gives him what he needs.

He tells Thomas, "Do not doubt but believe" (John 20:27). There was nothing about doubting, nothing about worthiness, and nothing about remedial school—just divine encouragement in lieu of empirical verification.

And what Jesus did for Thomas he does for you, for me, and for all people who may never think to even darken the door of a church. One concept we sometimes hear is that God pursues us. Even when we doubt, even when we are faithless, even when we choose not to believe, God pursues us. He encourages us and gives us what we need to believe. And then he waits . . . he waits for us to receive, to respond, to believe.

Thomas's reaction is both shocking and explicit: "My Lord and my God!" (John 20:28). In John's Gospel, Thomas is the only character to give this powerful and complete confession of faith. In fact, in all the Gospels, Thomas is the only person to link Jesus to God, Son, Father, Lord and God as *one*—one person. Thomas, having seen, not only believes but professes his belief. This is the climax of the Gospel. Remember the opening line of the Gospel of John? "In the beginning was the Word, and the Word was with

God, and the Word was God" (John 1:1). And remember what John writes near the end of his Gospel? "These [stories of Jesus] are written so that you may come to believe that Jesus is the Messiah, the Son of God, and that through believing you may have life in his name" (John 20:31). It's Thomas who puts it all together for us.

Here is one final thought. It was not Thomas touching Jesus that drew him to belief; it was Jesus's offering of himself, the invitation to Thomas to use whatever means necessary to come to faith. Jesus is not shaming Thomas, and he's not being sarcastic with Thomas. As he has done to others before and as he does for us today, Jesus gave Thomas everything he needed for faith.

During communion, we are given a small piece of bread and a sip of wine. The *Book of Common Prayer* calls these "the spiritual food of the most precious Body and Blood of your Son our Savior Jesus Christ."[1] This is an invitation for us here and now and every time we come together to bless the bread and drink the cup, to have faith rather than unfaith. That faith allows us to experience the climax of the gospel. That faith encourages us to see ourselves united with Jesus, his disciples, and all those in every generation who have looked to Jesus in hope. Just as Thomas was with Jesus and his eyes were opened so he no longer needed to touch Jesus's wounds. And so Jesus gives us everything we need to see *beyond* our need for *empirical verification*. Jesus tells us this when he says to his followers, "Blessed are those who have not seen [Jesus physically] and yet have come to believe" (John 20:29). That blessed, divine encouragement moves us by faith alone to take the final step to see, to believe, and to exclaim, "My Lord and my God!"

May we not be unbelieving, but believing.

---

1. *Book of Common Prayer*, 1979, 365.

Already, Not Yet

John 13:31–35, Revelation 21:1–6

In the Name of the Father, and of the Son, and of the Holy Spirit. Amen.

L et's consider the word *advent*. A good definition of *advent* is "a coming into place, or view, or being; an arrival."[1] Most Christians celebrate the season of Advent that begins about four weeks before Christmas Day. It is a time when we mark and remember prophecies about the coming Messiah, hear about John the Baptist, and remember the message of Gabriel to Mary that she would become the Theotokos—the God-bearer. However, the first Sunday of Advent usually has readings from the Gospel that depict the end of the world, or the end of days.

---

1. *Webster's Encyclopedic Unabridged Dictionary of the English Language* (1989), s.v. "Advent."

Our passage from Revelation is the beginning of the final "things"—a new heaven and a new earth, a city descending out of heaven, God wiping away tears, and water coming from a spring that is the water of life. These are strange images—images that are hard to wrap our minds around. Revelation is a hard book to understand, and it takes much exploration and study to wrestle with it. But for right now, remember this phrase: already, but not yet—things that are accomplished but not quite finished. This is a good starting place anytime we start discussing Revelation.

One thing to remember about the Book of Revelation is that it is not just pointing to the future; it is also a story about what is happening now, both in heaven and on earth. However, it was also written for first-century Christians to give them encouragement and strength as they endured persecution at the hands of the Roman Empire. Using these images and metaphors, John the Revelator gives his readers a glimpse of the glory that both is and is to come. We pick up the story at the climax. The whole saga of the Bible—from creation, captivity, and exile to Jesus's life, death, resurrection, and ascension, and to the work of the apostles in Acts—all of these point to the moment when heaven and earth are joined and become inseparable. This is not a destruction of the earth or a diminishing of heaven but a fulfillment of how God intended creation to be from the very beginning. Just prior to this passage in Revelation 20, we read that death and Hades, the final and most powerful enemies, are thrown into the lake of fire, a poetic way of saying that death is annihilated. The Apostle Paul speaks of this: "The last enemy to be destroyed is death" (1 Cor. 15:26). This is the culmination of all the work of God. At long last, God, his creation, and all the saints are together without death, pain, fear, worry, or doubt. And together, God dwells with them. The New Testament for Everyone translation of Revelation 21:3

reads like this: "Look! God has come to dwell with humans! He will dwell with them, and they will be his people, and God himself will be with them and will be their God." And this is already happening. Already . . .

. . . but not yet. We are still here on earth. We still experience death. We still have pain, fear, worry, and doubt. We still have sin. We still see evil all around us. We are in a permanent quasi-Advent season while we are here on earth. We are waiting, expecting, and longing for this new heaven to come into view and to see this earth restored as a new earth. And what are we supposed to do while we wait?

I think we can draw a clue from our Gospel of John passage: "I give you a new commandment, that you love one another. Just as I have loved you, you also should [perhaps *must* is a better word] love one another" (John 13:34). While Jesus says this is a new commandment, the strange thing is that this commandment is not new at all. We only have to turn back to Leviticus to see that God gave this commandment to Moses: "You shall not take vengeance or bear a grudge against any of your people, but you shall love your neighbor as yourself: I am the LORD" (Lev. 19:18).

So why does Jesus say that this is a "new" commandment? Perhaps this part of the phrase is key: "Just as I have loved you." Love your neighbor—love as I have loved. What does Jesus's love look like? In John 4, we meet a woman who has had one, two, three, four, five husbands, and she is still searching for true love. Jesus sits with her, talks to her, tells her the water of life will heal her, and loves her. And then there is the tax collector Zacchaeus who is perched in a tree. Luke's Gospel tells us that Zacchaeus's neighbors and countrymen hate him because he works for the occupiers—Rome. And what does Jesus do? He calls out to Zacchaeus and tells him that he wants to have dinner at his house, fellowship with him, and be his friend. Jesus recognizes, acknowledges, and loves him. And what happens? That love compels Zacchaeus to quit committing fraud and quit stealing from his neighbors, and he gives back four times the amount he has stolen from his community. There is also the demoniac who Jesus sails across the sea to rid of the legion of demons, even though everyone else is terrified of the man and has attempted to chain him up for his own good. What about the woman with the issue of blood or the widow who lost her only son? What about Lazarus who Jesus raised from the dead after four days and restored him to his sisters who were weeping when Jesus calls Lazarus out of the tomb? Or what about Peter who denies Jesus three times in a matter of hours?

And what about Judas? Jesus walked with him. Jesus talked with him. They ate together. They were part of a group of close friends who traveled around Galilee and came to Jerusalem for festivals. And Jesus washed his feet, called him friend, gave him a morsel of bread, knew what Judas was about to do, and told him to go and do it quickly. "So, after receiving the piece of bread, he immediately went out. And it was night" (John 13:30). And Jesus, who demonstrated all this love, who acted out true godly love, then tells his disciples to love one another—Judas included—as he has loved them. That is what love looks like when God dwells with us.

So what does loving one another as Jesus loves us look like right here, right now? It isn't just about coming within the walls of the church to say we love each other as we pass the peace. No, it's about what it looks like out there so we can help usher in this new heaven and this new earth and be part of that transforming power. It is here already, but not yet!

So let me ask you this: what does love, true Christian love, look like? What does it look like at the grocery store when the person ahead of you is struggling with children and can't find the money to buy the groceries she has in her basket (she's just a little short)? What does it look like when we interact with our coworkers or our customers? What does it look like when our civic clubs meet? What does the love of Jesus look like in our politics? Do we really need one more Facebook post or Twitter comment about how ugly or stupid someone is or how someone needs to go to prison, all because we simply don't agree with them politically?

What does the love of Jesus look like when our friends hurt us, a rift opens up and it seems like the personal relationship is in danger? What does the love of Jesus look like to the poor who are just down the street and live next door to us? What does it look like when we fear or question someone because they speak differently, have a different culture, or are simply a different color than we are? And what does the love of Jesus look like when a stranger sits down in our pew because they are out of options, are on the verge of giving up, and don't know where else to go? What does the love of Jesus look like when we really believe God dwells with us, cares for us, and wipes every tear from every eye?

I give you a *new* commandment . . . and I saw a new heaven and a new earth.

It is coming, and it is here—already, but not quite yet.[2]

---

2. Some of this sermon, particularly the litany of episodes of Jesus demonstrating love to those he encountered and ending with the love he also gave to Judas, comes from ideas in a sermon by the Reverend David Chalk, currently rector of St. Francis by the Lake in Canyon Lake, Texas. As I prepared to preach this sermon, I asked him if I could borrow his thoughts, for which he kindly gave me permission. So please know that Father Chalk had a rather significant hand in the preparation of this sermon. Thank you, David.

Mary and Martha

Luke 10:38–42

In the Name of the Father, and of the Son, and of the
Holy Spirit. Amen.

I f anyone ever asks me how I am doing, one of my typical
responses of late is, "Busy, but good." Probably all of us would
agree that we are busy—busy shuttling kids or grandkids to
soccer, camp, school; busy taking our parents to the doctor; busy
with work; busy at home; busy with our sports leagues—we are
just busy people!

In our story in Luke, Jesus is visiting a certain house as he jour-
neys to Jerusalem. And of course, when Jesus, the itinerant rabbi
and the talk of the countryside, is coming to stay in your home, you
need to get everything just right. You have food to prepare, rooms
to make ready, guests to invite, floors to sweep, laundry to do, and
tables to clean. Enter Martha—the original Martha Stewart. Martha is busy. She is anxious, worried, distracted, and troubled.

In contrast to Martha, her sister Mary is not holding up her end of the bargain and is actually bringing shame to the house. How is that? Simple—she is listening to the rabbi. She is sitting at Jesus's feet listening to what he says, and women did not do that sort of thing in first-century Palestine.

Sitting at the feet of Jesus is not a picturesque image of a devoted Mary hanging onto every word Jesus utters. Rather, it connotes a sense of intense learning. To sit at the feet of a rabbi meant you wanted to become a rabbi yourself. Some of us have "sat at the feet" of instructors to become lawyers, doctors, businesspeople, musicians, or artists. And many times, those instructors or mentors told us after a lesson to "go and do likewise."

Go and do likewise. Have you heard that recently? In Luke 10, we find the parable of the Good Samaritan, a man who stopped to help an injured man on the side of the road. Listening to that story, we sometimes lose the sense that the story is a lesson. The command of Jesus at the end is to "go and do likewise" (Luke 10:37), which means we are to show mercy to our neighbor.

Luke wrote these two passages—Mary and Martha and the Good Samaritan—to follow each other. If we were to read the Gospel continuously, we would finish the Good Samaritan passage and immediately find ourselves in Mary and Martha's house. When Luke writes this way—juxtaposing two seemingly unrelated passages—he is hinting at a larger lesson, a both-and lesson. You can't separate the two stories.

Jesus's rebuke of Martha has been read and taught as a rebuke of being too busy—of overdoing her work or perhaps being too extravagant with the guest in her house. Mary, on the other hand, is praised for being passive, listening, and contemplating what she is hearing. But neither extreme is right when you isolate them. Martha is so busy *doing* her job that she has forgotten *how* to do her job. Instead of being a good hostess, which was her aim, she actually puts Jesus on the spot. "Lord, do you not care? . . . Tell her then to help me!" (Luke 10:40). She presumes to tell her Lord what to do! Against that is Jesus's comment about Mary choosing the "better part" (Luke 10:42). She is listening and learning; she is becoming a disciple. It is Martha's lack of focus, not her busyness, that is the problem. What Jesus tells us in the parable of the Good Samaritan and what we see in the story of Mary and Martha is to listen, learn, and then go and do likewise.

Following Christ and being a Christian and a disciple are always best when there is a balance. Prayer and study are only effective when also accompanied by service and action. Service and action are only focused and in harmony with each other when they are rooted in prayer and study. For too long, the church has seen Martha as being chided by Jesus, but Jesus is calling her attention into focus. It is not the work she is doing that is the problem. It is the worry and trouble that accompany the work. Martha is at the party but is not actively in the party. Jesus her Lord is in her home, but she is too busy to stop and listen.

As the Roman Empire was collapsing and falling into the hands of the vandals and barbarians, Benedict of Nursia decided to leave Rome and move into a cave on a hillside about 40 miles away. There, after two attempts, he founded what is now called the Benedictine Order, the oldest Western-based monastic community where he devised both a rule and a motto. The rule was about how to live life in community with others, prescribing everything from when the monks should pray, work, and eat along with how to do all the mundane daily tasks communal life requires. But the motto of the Order sums up the rule *Ora et Labora*—prayer and work. What Benedict attempted to do was simple: compose a treatise on balance. The trick is to actually live life in that balance.

I imagine the story of Mary and Martha was on Benedict's mind often during those years.

We as the church are a community as well. We pray together. We make Eucharist together. We fellowship together. We work together. We celebrate together. We mourn together. So how do we work to achieve a healthy balance as a community? Let me give you three ideas to ponder.

First, we need to recall our Baptismal Covenant, or the vows each of us take when we are baptized and renew from time to time. In those vows, we see what our mission is in this life. The first of these is to continue in the apostles' teaching and fellowship, in the breaking of bread, and in prayers. That is Mary in our study. And this is what we do every time we gather for the celebration of the Eucharist. But take note: since it is the first, that makes it the most important of the vows. Now, what follows? The answer is everything we do the next six days. Do we resist evil? Do we proclaim the gospel by word and example? Do we seek to serve Christ in all persons? Do we strive for justice and respect the dignity of our neighbors? That is Martha. And it is the Good Samaritan. You see, we cannot do the work of God in this world unless we are empowered by the teachings of the apostles, unless we are doing the work with prayer, unless we are in fellowship with others, and unless we understand the sacramental nature of life. *Ora et Labora*: prayer and work.

This is why the church is in a troubled spot and why that trouble is a good and holy thing. The church is on the decline in many places around the globe, particularly in North America and Europe, both of which were former bastions of Christendom. Why? We can blame many things, from the preaching to the music to the building to the style of worship to the grumpy old people to the need for added excitement. And some of that may play a part. But I am convinced that we as the church have been Martha for too long. We have had programs, drives, capital campaigns, new worship styles, projectors, rock bands, and Starbucks in the narthex. The list could go on and on, but rarely do we center those programs and tasks in prayer. Neither do we center our mundane and daily tasks in prayer. This is a call to everyone— not just the rector. It includes the vestry and governing bodies, school boards that are attached to churches, guilds and groups such as the Daughters of the King or the parish choir that meets with a purpose, and on and on. It continues until we reach the point where you and I, both corporately and individually, must pray about the needs of the church daily. The answer is simple. We are the holy church of God, and we don't have a balance of prayer, fellowship, and Eucharist. Globally, we don't live up to the first of our vows in our covenant.[1]

Second, we as Western Christians are extremely good at making commitments, particularly at committing to something other than making time for God on Sundays. It is much easier to sleep in because it is our only day off. It is more fun to be hunting than giving up a few hours in the morning to attend Mass. We take our kids to their soccer game on Sunday morning rather than tell the coaches that sports are important, but God comes first. We have relegated what we profess to believe to the second- or third-chair position. Why? Some would answer that we don't "get anything out of church" or "I can find God in nature" (or

---

1. The Baptismal Covenant this section refers to can be found on pages 304 and 305 of the *Book of Common Prayer*, 1979. This covenant includes the vows we take to live out our calling and our lives as Christians. They are professed at each service where baptism occurs but also from time to time on special days such as Easter Eve, All Saints Day, Pentecost, and the Feast of the Baptism of our Lord.

fill in the blank). In truth, those statements may be 100 percent accurate, but isn't that like Martha asking Jesus to do something rather than listening and learning?

Third, one of the elements that keeps the church in unity with itself is communion, Holy Eucharist. The sacrament of Eucharist is literally bread for our journey each week. The reason we make Eucharist each week is akin to the reason we literally eat each day—we must have food to continue to live, to work, and to survive. And that is where we meet Jesus. The disciples knew the Lord Jesus in the breaking of the bread. You see, when we gather together, we *are* the body of Christ. And as the body of Christ, we *share* in the body and blood of Christ. That sharing empowers us to *be* the body of Christ in the world. That is our "Mary moment," enabling us to be a Martha without distraction, anxiety, worry, or trouble in the world. That is how we achieve the balance we need.

Let me offer you a few questions to ask and ponder. Am I Mary, or am I Martha? What do I need to do to balance my life? What are my commitments and priorities? What makes me anxious day to day? What will I learn if I sit at the feet of my Lord and then go and do likewise?

Money Bins and Silos

Luke 12:13–21

*In the Name of the Father, and of the Son, and of the
Holy Spirit. Amen.*

There once was an extremely wealthy duck who not only
had quite a bit of money but also had his own highly
secured money bin. Scrooge McDuck's money bin was 13
stories tall, 11 of which contained a vast area that held the cash
and coins he had accumulated over the course of his lifetime—
approximately three cubit acres of cash (the value was almost
incalculable). The stories in *DuckTales*, a cartoon from my youth,
were either stories of McDuck and his nephews, Huey, Dewey,
and Louie, on some globe-trotting adventure (when he wasn't too
busy with his favorite pastime—swimming in his money) or of
someone itching to get Scrooge's money. Part of the plot was not

only how these villains were attempting to steal the money but also what lengths McDuck would go to so his money was secure. There were lasers, snakes, bear traps, impaling rods, walls that would crush you if you entered a code incorrectly. All of them were there to protect the most valued possession in Scrooge's life—his money and his first dime—which was housed in a little shrine inside the money bin.

At some level, I think all of us have our Scrooge McDuck habits—maybe not swimming in money but perhaps forming little shrines to the important and valuable possessions in our lives, shrines we attempt to render impenetrable. The parable about the rich man in our reading is hard to grasp, partly because it is short but also because some of what Jesus is talking about sounds good. Let's deconstruct some of it and see what we find.

First, the rich man is a farmer of sorts. He has land, barns, and an abundant supply of produce from a harvest. He has produced a bumper crop. In Judaism, one of the many ways God blesses you is with abundance—plenty of cash, crops, and land, among other things. Prosperity is considered a blessing from God. Think of Job who was wealthy and successful and had a large family. One of the psalms asks for such a blessing: "May our barns be filled to overflowing with all manner of crops; may the flocks in our pastures increase by thousands and tens of thousands; may our cattle be fat and sleek." (Ps. 144:13–14 Book of Common Prayer). How many of us who have land, crops, and cattle pray this very prayer every day? In essence, many people would look upon this man and say something to this effect: "Well, God has certainly blessed him!" And they would be right.

Next, let's look at what the rich man feels he needs to do. He needs to store his crop, but he doesn't have room in his barns. So he proceeds to raze the barns he has in order to build even larger barns to store his crops. That was very prudent—larger crops, larger barns—and who knows, perhaps next year's crop will be even better. Planning for the future is always sound financial advice. Let's think back to Genesis and the story of Joseph, the slave, who interprets Pharaoh's dream and subsequently becomes a prince of Egypt. Joseph tells Pharaoh to "take one-fifth of the produce of the land" (Gen. 41:34) and gather it up as a reserve. Genesis even says this: "Joseph stored up grain in such abundance—like the sand of the sea—that he stopped measuring it; it was beyond measure" (Gen. 41:49).

Third and finally, the rich man is so confident he will be well off for many years that he is ready to eat, drink, and be merry. He has done well for himself. He has achieved financial security for the rest of his days, and he is ready to retire. Now that God has blessed him beyond measure, he is ready to reap the benefits of that blessing.

So what is the problem? What is Jesus drawing our attention to? Maybe we ought to examine what Jesus is *not* saying. First, Jesus is not saying that having an abundance is wrong. This is not a call to sell everything you own and live as a pauper. Second, Jesus is not saying that being rich is a sin, although in this and other passages, he does say that having riches on earth can put a strain on your priorities. Third, Jesus is not saying that celebrating events or blessings on this earth is akin to haughtiness or in some way a wrong way to celebrate, be it holidays, birthdays, closing a major deal, or getting a raise at work. Don't forget about the woman at a dinner party who broke out the expensive perfume and anointed Jesus while Judas complained that the money could have been given to the poor. Celebration is part of life, and Jesus certainly went to many parties and even partied with sinners.

Greed is the problem Jesus is addressing in this parable. Greed is not about having things, and it is not about a certain socioeconomic class. There are both rich and poor people who are greedy. Greed isn't even expressing an honest need for something such as food, shelter, or clothing. Instead, greed is an excessive desire, an inordinate focus on getting more, sometimes more than your actual fair share. Many times it has to do with wealth, how much more we want to make, even if we are dishonest in our methods. Often, it has to do with stuff—I will only be happy if I can get this one more thing, and I might even want to prevent anyone else from having it.

Greed is one of those sins that is not focused on one thing but is wide-ranging. Greed for food, money, status, or power can destroy our inner self. It is almost like possessing a ring that becomes "your precious" and turns you into a shadow of your former self, like Gollum in J. R. R. Tolkien's *The Lord of the Rings*. As Saint Thomas Aquinas pointed out, "Greed is a sin against God, just as all mortal sins, in as much as man condemns things eternal for the sake of temporal things."[1] Gordon Gekko in the film *Wall Street* tells us that greed is good, and as the movie shows, it was good enough to land Gekko in prison.

This may beg the question, what is the remedy for greed?

Let's go back to the story again and reexamine our rich friend. He has an abundance of grain or some other commodity. But what does he do with that abundance? Does he contemplate sharing it perhaps with the workers who harvested the grain for him? No. Does he follow the Law and the prophets' teachings and share with widows or orphans? No. Does he sell some of his abundance

---

1. "All Thomas Aquinas Quotes about 'Sin,'" *Inspiring Quotes*, https://www.inspiringquotes.us/author/9350-thomas-aquinas/about-sin.

and use the money to aid the poor around him? No. Instead, the imagination of his heart is about the new problem he has, and his harvest is a problem, not a blessing.

He then turns to the barns, and since those aren't big enough to hold his harvest, he destroys them and builds new, bigger ones. Imagine this: a local farmer harvests his grain, and since it is a great year, he tears down his silos, lets the grain sit outside, and waits for the new silos to be built. We would probably look at him and ask ourselves if he had lost his mind because surely some, if not all, of the grain will mildew or become infested with bugs while he builds his new silos. But since his old silos can't hold all the grain, no one else gets to share in the abundance.

Third, and this is perhaps the most insidious of all, the rich man and his possessions become the focus of his life. Notice that he and the crop are the only characters in this story, and everything is I, me, and my. His new focus then leads him to hedonism—relax, drink, eat, and be merry because you have no more cares or worries in this world. Nowhere does our friend say, "Let me invite my friends over to celebrate and share with them." Nowhere does our friend turn to those in need and say, "Let me share with you out of my many blessings." Nowhere does our friend say, "I wonder if my friend or my neighboring farmer needs some grain to get through the year."

God's declaration of "you fool!" (Luke 12:20) has everything to do with the rich man's thoughts. He has forgotten that nothing is his eternally—only temporarily. Recall Thomas Aquinas and how we condemn things eternal for things temporal. Luke's Gospel is constantly reminding us that things are not always as they seem. Remember the *Magnificat*, the Song of Mary: "He hath shewed strength with his arm; he hath scattered the proud in the imagination of their hearts. He hath put down the might from their seats, and exalted them of low degree. He hath filled the hungry with good things; and the rich he hath sent empty away" (Luke 1:51–53 KJV). It is cliché to say, but our friend has forgotten that all the stuff, all the possessions, all the wealth—well, you can't take them with you.

There is a word we use to describe a remedy: *stewardship*. We must understand that we are only stewards—caretakers, if you will—of all we have and all we have received. Stewardship is about setting our possessions in right alignment. Stewardship is about caring for ourselves and our families, our friends, our neighbors, and ultimately the world around us. Stewardship is rendering thanks to God by acknowledging that all we are blessed with is a gift—not a problem. When we align our thinking and our focus on the stuff we have and the money we make and attempt to find a why to give God the glory for these gifts, that is when we store up treasures and find ourselves rich toward God.

Don't be like Scrooge McDuck who worries, frets, and goes to elaborate measures just to protect his money. Don't be like a Gollum who is so consumed with a possession that it physically changes him into a monster. Don't be like Gordon Gekko who justified as good what he knew to be harmful to himself and those around him. Don't be like the rich man who gave in to hedonism and cared for no one but himself.

Rather, be like Joseph who prudently saved and was able to provide not just for Egypt but ultimately for his family in Canaan. Be like Job who even in the dark days of ruin, death, and illness continued to bless God. Be like someone you know who is generous, shares, and thinks of others. Become someone who shares abundantly and is rich toward his neighbors and God.

Finding the Lost Sheep

Luke 15:1–10

In the Name of the Father, and of the Son, and of the
Holy Spirit. Amen.

I must have been about six or seven when my mother decided we should take a trip to San Antonio, Texas, for the day. One of the highlights of the trip was a stop at the Tower of the Americas in Hemisfair Park just south of downtown San Antonio. Unknown to me at the time, my mother was deathly afraid of heights, so the elevator ride (enclosed by glass on all sides so you could see well) was terrifying for her. We skipped the revolving restaurant and went up to the observation deck where we could circumnavigate the tower as well as step outside to a highly secure breezeway. We had probably been at the literal top of San Antonio for about five minutes when my mother said, "You stay right here. I'll be right back." And she proceeded to the ladies' room.

I was now stationed in front of the ladies' room like a sentry, and from there I couldn't see anything. I couldn't look out, I couldn't see the skyline. All I could see was a mass of people walking past me. I decided to leave my assigned post and walk (in my mind) about 20 feet or so to where I could see and have a better vantage point. After a few minutes, I realized three things: (1) when I turned around, I had absolutely no idea where I had come from, (2) I had no idea where my mother was, and (3) I was utterly lost, having not ventured 20 feet but probably a good quarter of the way around the tower. What I did not know was that I had given my mother a shock, and she was beginning to fear I had been kidnapped or perhaps even something worse. Long story short, I stood still in my fright, and my mother traversed the tower, eventually finding me, both of us relieved.

All of us have lost something, and many or perhaps all of us have been lost. Hopefully, we have all experienced the joy of being found or finding what we have lost. Jesus has given us two parables in quick succession in this passage in Luke. Each one is about someone losing something. In the first parable, a shepherd has lost his sheep. He rather recklessly leaves the rest of his flock in the wilderness where anything from wolves to thieves can kill or steal them in order to look for one little sheep. If you think about it in economies of scale, the shepherd left behind his investment, or the investment of his master, to look for something of little value.

In the second parable, we meet a woman who has lost a silver coin. The coin is not worth a whole lot, only about a day's wages. But she literally tears the house apart looking for it, much like taking a flashlight and looking under the sofa for the keys you lost. Rather than saying, "it will turn up when it turns up," she sweeps diligently throughout the house.

Both the shepherd and the woman search and seek until they find what they are looking for. But what else do they do? They call their friends and neighbors and throw a party to celebrate recovering what they lost. You can imagine that the expense of throwing the party is probably more than the cost of the lost sheep or coin.

What Jesus is doing here is setting up an argument that works two ways. First, God is both the shepherd and the woman, each searching diligently for something he or she has lost. In one case, the sheep may have wandered off, and in the other, the coin may have fallen off a table or into a crack. There's one thing to know about sheep. When they are lost, they don't cry out but instead hunker down and freeze with fear, making the search all the more difficult. In like manner, a lost coin can't call out and help the seeker find it. Both the sheep and the coin are powerless to help themselves; they need to be rescued.

Second, we have Jesus talking to the Pharisees and teachers who are grumbling. What's the problem? Jesus is treating everyone (sinners and tax collectors) like equals. He is giving them a place to exist, a place to be listened to, and a place to fellowship—and he eats with them. Jesus is hanging out with all the wrong sorts of people. And the Pharisees (who are the 99 righteous sheep in the first parable) aren't rejoicing. They're grumbling. Rather than being thankful someone else is doing this work of teaching so they don't have to get their hands dirty, they're halfway upset that these *sinners* might learn something, maybe become part of their fellowship, and become *like them*. Jesus has searched them out and brought these worthless sinners in. He has found his lost sheep and his lost coin.

You see, God is constantly searching out people—his people. As we already discussed, God pursues us. Even when we doubt, even when we are faithless, and even when we choose not to believe, God pursues us. When the world, our friends, or even our own selves say we are worthless and lost, God still pursues us. Jesus modeled that pursuit—we call it love.

Yes, God pursues us. But—and this is crucial—God wants us to join him in that pursuit. That is what living as a Christian means, to not sit back and dream of a better world but to take an active role in shaping it. It is not wondering who is going to help the poor and the needy as a group, but it is helping the one individual you encounter—perhaps even at a most unwelcomed moment in time. And God invites us to join not only in the pursuit but in the festivities when we see lives recovered.

What does joining in a pursuit with God look like in your hometown?

Your church may already do much work and outreach with your community, but there is always that one lost sheep, that one lost coin that needs to be found. You and I have been that sheep or that coin, and we know what it means to be found and to be pursued. Therefore, we must not flag or fail—the work never ends! Just imagine the rejoicing in heaven when we join in God's holy pursuit.

Remembering the Human Element

Luke 17:11–19

*In the Name of the Father, and of the Son, and of the
Holy Spirit, Amen.*

One morning while I was surfing through my Facebook account, a headline grabbed my attention, so much that I stopped my mindless scrolling and clicked to read the article. *Business Insider* had an article about a CEO with a rather unusual if not extremely time-consuming habit. Here's the headline that stopped me: "A CEO Who Writes 9,200 Employee Birthday Cards a Year Explains the Value of Gratitude." The article explored Sheldon Yellen of Belfor Holdings, Inc. and his commitment to writing cards to his employees on their birthdays to express his gratitude to each individual for the work they do at the company. They were all handwritten cards—no two alike. And no, his secretary didn't do it for him.

When Yellen travels, he is known to take a suitcase with him full of stationery and pens, sometimes spending the entire flight writing these birthday cards. In fact, he doesn't stop there. He also writes thank you notes, anniversary cards, and holiday cards. And if he happens to hear that an employee's child is sick, he takes the time to scribble out a get well soon card and send it to the ailing child. When an interviewer asked him why he continues this gesture that many other CEOs or managers may find a complete waste of time, Yellen said this in response: "When leaders forget about the human element, they're holding back their companies and limiting the success of others. Focusing only on profit and forgetting that a company's most important asset is its people will ultimately stifle a company's growth."[1]

When we forget about the human element . . .

Ten lepers make an appearance in our Gospel reading. In the ancient world, leprosy was a chronic infectious disease of the skin and sometimes nerves and other parts of the body. The disease rendered someone "unclean." Being unclean was not a matter of simply being dirty as in covered in mud or oil and not allowed into the house until you washed. Being unclean was both a social and a religious status. Someone who was unclean was cut off from society, not allowed to participate in the life of the community and forbidden from touching another human being. Unless proof was given to a priest that a person had indeed been made clean, even the religious authorities of the day

---

1. Allana Akhtar, "A CEO Who Writes 9,200 Employee Holiday Cards a Year Explains the Value of Gratitude," *Business Insider*, December 24, 2019, https://www.businessinsider.com/ceo-writes-7400-employee-birthday-cards-each-year-2017-6.

ostracized them. There were many activities that were part of life that could render a person unclean, but the majority of these unclean activities required either a ritual cleansing or a period of time to pass before a priest pronounced the person clean. Not so with leprosy.

Leprosy was for all practical purposes a death sentence, both figuratively and actually in some cases. Lepers could not live in their city, and eventually colonies of these "walking dead" sprang up. They had to call out "unclean" to anyone they saw, thereby giving voice to this dark, depressing reality every day. Can you imagine the psychological impact of having to denounce yourself daily to people around you? Lepers could not interact with people they knew and loved. In fact, the fear was so intense that someone standing in the shadow of a leper could also be declared unclean. They were no longer part of any meaningful community. They were *excommunicated*. Notice that our 10 lepers follow the custom of the day: "Keeping their distance, they called out" (Luke 17:12–13).

This passage is somewhat unique since in many ways Jesus is not the main character. It is a leper, and not only a leper who has been healed but a person who is a foreigner—a Samaritan, the most unlikely of people in this story.

Another aspect that makes this story unique is the questions it leaves for the reader. What happened to the other nine? Were they so overwhelmed that they lost sight of what they had just received? Or was it a lack of attention? Had they not noticed the change in themselves like the Samaritan had? Or perhaps it was a matter of priorities. Maybe they needed to see their families and friends first before they made their way to the priests.

What the leper received from Jesus was more than the cure of a skin disease. As hideous and painful as the physical ailment of leprosy was, the more lasting healing was a chance for restoration in his community. Rather than being a "walking dead man" among all the people he knew, he was given new life. Rather than having to cry out "unclean" to all who approached, his new cry became "Hallelujah! Praise the Lord!" In healing the leper, our Lord restored someone to a full state of humanity.

All of us in the United States are fortunate people. If you live in the United States, you are among the wealthiest people on the planet. Even the poor in our communities rarely face the abject poverty many in other nations face. With that in mind, let me ask a question. What are you thankful for? Be honest with yourself; you don't have to give a Sunday school answer. For some of us, it might be good health. For others, it may be the love of friends and family. Many of us might say it's the joy that children or grandchildren provide us. Some of us might recount an experience, the time the world seemed to be falling apart before our eyes, and somehow we pulled through it. A few of us might consider an achievement such as finding a job or earning a diploma as something we are thankful for. Perhaps yesterday's college football game even played out the way we had hoped!

Stewardship is all about gratitude. It is about expressing to God a profound sense of joy and thankfulness for all we have, all we are, and all our potential can be. Sometimes we express this as being stewards of our time, talents, and treasures. And yes, that is true. But we are called to be stewards of everything—all of creation. Stewardship and gratitude are about how we spend our lives. Our friend the leper understood this, which is why he not only fell prostrate at our Lord's feet but also praised God out loud for anyone and everyone to hear.

Living a life of gratitude is one way we can put all things in perspective. A term one of my college professors often repeated was that thanksgiving is shown by *thanks-living*.[2] Living into a life that renders thanks to God in all aspects is something that takes work, practice, recognition, and focus.

Practicing gratitude is both simple and hard. It is simple in that practice makes it easier. When do you express gratitude to people around you? Is it the server who brings you more water, coffee, or tea? Do you tell the person checking out your groceries that you appreciate them, or do you complain that there aren't enough sackers to bag your groceries? What about the people who do the tasks and chores they are supposed to do? Perhaps if all of us, employees and customers alike, showed and practiced gratitude a little more in just one aspect, it would spill over into others' lives.

Showing gratitude is hard. It requires us to look beyond ourselves and actually see the people around us, what they do, and how they contribute to the world. Sheldon Yellen understands that very clearly, that no one is beyond his sight. He does the hard work of sitting down to write his expressions of gratitude and thanksgiving to his employees. Acknowledging the human elements around us is one of the hardest skills to develop, but with a little practice each day, all of us can develop, grow, and nurture that way of life.

Here are some words from the Prayer of General Thanksgiving: "We bless thee for our creation, preservation, and all the blessings of this life; but above all, for Thine inestimable love [I love that word *inestimable*] in the redemption of the

---

2. One of my esteemed professors and mentors, the Reverend Dr. Terry York, uses this phrase when he teaches some of his classes. His commitment to this concept is so firm that he wrote a hymn that was published in the 1991 edition of *The Baptist Hymnal*, included as hymn number 642, *Thanksgiving/Thanks-living*.

world by our Lord Jesus Christ, for the means of grace, and for the hope of glory."[3]

Start today. Take one or two steps. Call or write someone because it is their birthday. Tell the person who serves you at the coffee shop thank you when they refill your cup, and mean it. Take time to look someone in the eye and express your gratitude that they are around. Take time to ponder what God has done in your life, and when you say your prayers, be certain to thank the Lord for his gifts to you and to this world.

---

3. "The General Thanksgiving," *Book of Common Prayer,* 1979, 71.

The Kingdom of God

Matthew 13:31–35

In the Name of the Father, and of the Son, and of the Holy Spirit. Amen.

Two words ring in my head when I read this passage in Matthew 13—*hidden* and *patience*. Hidden is the mustard seed that must be planted in the ground, covered with dirt, and invisible to our eyes. Patience is that we must wait, and the process of waiting, especially for something like the growth of a small tree, is sometimes slower than we would like. The same is true for yeast added to dough. If dough is mixed well, you can't grab a portion of it and say, "Here is the yeast." Rather, it is incorporated into the whole, and that yeast affects the entirety of the dough into which it is placed. Once again, the baker must wait and have patience for the dough to rise or else the bread will be flat and tough.

Other than agricultural and cooking tips, what is Jesus trying to tell his disciples and us? Notice that these comparative parables all refer back to this phrase: "The kingdom of heaven is like. . . ." Like trees and dough? Yes, actually, exactly like that.

Jesus is telling his disciples that God's kingdom is breaking into the world and that breaking into the world is a gradual process. It is something that takes time and is generally unseen until it is accomplished. Each year I plant a small garden from seeds, and each year I am amazed that within a few days of planting, many of the seeds have already sprouted roots and leaves, seemingly overnight. But then, we must still wait for those plants to bear fruit. We must have patience during the growing. We must wait for the fruit to ripen.

God's creation, from the first days until now, is a series of processes we all must endure. Remember, Jesus wasn't born as a fully grown man. He had to live the fullness of a human life—be born, grow, experience a normal human life, and ultimately die—until the work of salvation, the bringing of the Kingdom, could occur.

What does bringing in the Kingdom look like? Another way to ask the question is this: where did you see God at work this week? On November 2nd each year, All Souls' Day occurs. This day was typically set aside to recognize the saints who were part of our lives, while November 1st, All Saints' Day, was given to the men and women the church officially recognized, or canonized, as saints.

I can think of several men and women, many the larger church wouldn't know, who were full of hope but also understood patience and waiting for God's Kingdom to come. We all know these people, and mine happen to be my mother's secretary, one of my doctoral professors, a member of the Altar Guild at Saint

Philip's, and a pro-football player turned insurance salesman who was an imperfect man but understood God's love and redemption better than anyone I know. These were people who showed me where God's Kingdom was poking through the earth or where bread was starting to rise.

The Kingdom of God is here already, but also not yet. The Kingdom is like the mustard tree but without fruit. The tree is growing and is green with leaves, but it just doesn't have its fullness of fruit yet. The Kingdom is also like the dough with yeast. It is rising and will be ready to bake in just a little while, but in the meantime, we must wait a bit. God's Kingdom has broken in, even though we may not be able to see it right now or see it all around us. It's hidden, but like so many things we cannot see, it is right there in front of us—all the time.

We must also remember that God's Kingdom might not be quite like we expect. Many of the followers of Jesus were expecting a revolutionary leader, a military commander who could eventually rout out Caesar and the forces of Rome. But Jesus's Kingdom, the Kingdom of heaven, looked vastly different from their expectations, and perhaps it will look different from ours as well.

So be patient and wait in the knowledge of God's redemption. Be on the lookout for things that are hidden or veiled from our sight.

Do Not Be Afraid

Isaiah 7:10–16 and Matthew 1:18–25

In the Name of the Father, and of the Son, and of the
Holy Spirit. Amen.

W hen Christmas rolls around each year, the hustle and bustle can sometimes create a more cynical approach to the season the closer it gets. If you are anything like me, Christmas comes just a little too quickly to put any thought behind a present for just about anyone. We can become worried, stressed, and depressed about all the plans for Christmas—who is coming, where we are going, how many presents we should buy for distant cousins, if there is a parking spot at the mall. And then there are the two people you will meet everywhere. One is a cross between Ebenezer Scrooge and the Grinch, and the other is the person who loves the season so much that they start wearing Santa Claus hats and putting reindeer antlers on their car as soon as they finish Thanksgiving Day lunch. It is exhausting and overwhelming, and sometimes I feel like Scrooge and just want to say, "Bah! Humbug!"

In the midst of seasons like that, our readings actually tell us to stop for a moment and look—really take a look at what is going on around us. You may be wondering what we are looking for. It's simple. We're looking for God's faithfulness—not our faithfulness or lack thereof to God, but God's faithfulness to us, his creation; God's faithfulness to Israel; and God's faithfulness to you, to me, to the church, and to the world.

In our Isaiah reading, King Ahaz is in an extremely precarious situation. Jerusalem is surrounded by an army, and the practice of siege warfare in those days was not so much to attack the city but to wait and starve the city out. Jerusalem is literally starving. Speaking through Isaiah, God basically says something like this: "Just ask me for proof, and I will give you whatever you need. It doesn't matter how simple or how difficult; let me prove my faithfulness to you." Can you imagine God saying to you, "I'm here. Tell me how I can show you that." Perhaps we are somewhat like Ahaz. Instead of welcoming that offer, we say (probably out of false piety), "Who am I to test God? Who am I to say to God, 'Prove to me your faithfulness'?"

But what does God do? He tells Ahaz it doesn't matter—that this is what to look for. And what is it? It is a pregnant woman. Now remember, Jerusalem is surrounded, people are about to starve, and God gives Ahaz a sign, a young woman who is with child. What on earth could that possibly mean? Usually when there are epidemics or massive famines, the first to die are the elderly and young children. They are the most vulnerable and also the ones who need the most care. God in his faithfulness is going to save Judah, the house of David. God is not abandoning his people. Isaiah is saying to King Ahaz that the child who is not yet born is going to live and grow and become a mature person. Think back to Abraham who was told that his descendants would be more numerous than the stars in the sky. Remember David (whose line King Ahaz came from) and the promise that God would never abandon his house? To Ahaz and all Jerusalem, things looked very dark, and death was literally at their doorstep. Ahaz needed to recognize the new life that is the promise of the covenants of old and trust in God's faithfulness.

Several centuries later, another descendant of the house of David enters our narrative in Matthew. His name is Joseph, and he is in a rather tricky spot. The woman to whom he is engaged appears to have slept with someone else before their marriage and is now pregnant. We have a scandal. In Joseph's time, this offense was punishable by death, but Joseph, who truly loves Mary and perhaps even wants her to be happy with her lover (that he only suspected she had), decides to quietly separate from her so it won't cause either of them any shame or disgrace. He has set in place a course of action that will be mutually beneficial. And what happens? An angel says to Joseph the critical words that almost every encounter with God or an angel seems to require—do not be afraid.

Do not be afraid. How often do we need to hear that? Do not be afraid. For some people, Christmas is especially troubling. Maybe their heart yearns and aches for loved ones who are gone either by death, distance, or relationships that have ended. For others, it is the fear that this is the last Christmas with their mother, father, spouse, or perhaps their own sick child. Do not be afraid. Perhaps it is the job that was lost just this week and the fear of disappointing the small children who expect Saint Nicholas to come down the chimney and make a Christmas array of gifts the eye has never seen. Do not be afraid. Or maybe it is the war veteran who is so ravaged by depression and PTSD that he hasn't been out in months and is so lost that he considers the unthinkable. Do not be afraid.

You see, the beginning of recognizing God's faithfulness is letting go of the fears that fog our vision. Joseph understands this and "did as the angel commanded." And in Matthew's Gospel, the image of that pregnant woman takes on a name—Mary. She is the bearer of Emmanuel—God with us.

When Ahaz looks on the young woman, God's faithfulness and the faith of man collide. When Joseph takes Mary, cares for her, and does as the angel bids him, God's faithfulness and the faith of man collide. When we look at situations in our own lives and take a step in faith, God's faithfulness and our own faith collide.

I have never liked the saying, "When God shuts a door, he opens another one." I have often thought it a petty saying because God really doesn't shut doors; he flings doors open. Yes, sometimes jobs or opportunities end. And yes, sometimes we need out of something like a bad relationship that is hurting us. But instead of God shutting a door, it is God moving us forward and demonstrating his faithfulness. When the darkest night is the reality we face, watch out! God's faithfulness is the dawn you see in the eastern sky. All you are required to do is trust. And maybe it isn't one door that opens but multiple doors or opportunities—such as God telling Ahaz to ask for a sign—no matter how big or small.

In the opening verses of the Gospel of Matthew, Matthew defines *Emmanuel:* God with us. Part of what Matthew and Isaiah are both trying to tell us is that God *is* with us. At the end of Matthew is a passage we call the Great Commission. In that wonderful verse are the final words of Jesus, our Emmanuel: "And, lo, *I am with you always,* even unto the end of the world" (emphasis added) (Matt. 28:20). Emmanuel, Jesus, the embodiment of God with us, is still God with us always.

Perhaps one of the greatest gifts we can give to those around us is to be the non-anxious presence in their lives. In a world filled with fear and despair, we desperately need to hear the words of calm and peace: "Do not be afraid." We as the church are to be a beacon of what God's faithfulness looks like. Think back to Moses and the deliverance at the Red Sea. What did he tell the children of Israel? "Do not be afraid, stand firm, and see the deliverance that the LORD will accomplish for you today" (Exod. 14:13). The entire Bible is filled with stories like this, and the critical thing to recognize is that God has never been unfaithful to anyone—not to Adam and Eve, not to Noah, not to Abraham, not to Joseph in Egypt, not to Moses, not to David, not to Ahaz, not to Joseph, not to Mary, not to Jesus on the cross, not to Peter and Paul, not to the other apostles, not to the saints and martyrs throughout the ages, not to you, and not to me. If God were ever unfaithful to just one person, he would cease to be a deity we could put our trust in.

Remember that Emmanuel came for us to be God with us. That is the sign of God's love and faithfulness. So look around for the signs of God's grace, mercy, and love. And above all, do not be afraid.

The Light of the World

John 1:1–18

In the Name of the Father, and of the Son, and of the
Holy Spirit. Amen.

Anyone who is either an expert in languages or is multilingual will probably understand the phrase "lost in translation." For example, when a joke or phrase has a completely different meaning in another language, we might say it was lost in translation. Anyone who has written an international bestseller knows that when their book is translated into other languages, one of the ways to ensure its success abroad is for foreign editors to take the book's jokes, passing phrases, or even implied sarcasm and edit them for the intended audience. For instance, in English we have two words that are not related at all: *room* and *carpenter*. However, in German, a room is a *zimmer* and a carpenter is a *zimmerman*—someone who builds rooms. Speaking in English, we would never say, "I need to hire a roomman." However, if you speak to someone in Germany, the relation makes perfect sense: If you need a *zimmer*, you should hire a *zimmerman*.

The prologue of John's Gospel is a spellbinding, mesmerizing, and other-worldly account of who Christ is. But when we read those 18 verses in English, much is lost in translation. There is a lot clouded in a fog of mystery in the opening phrase, "In the beginning was the Word" (John 1:1). Ever since the Venerable Bede in the early eighth century tried his hand at translating the Gospel of John into English, this prologue has been a problem. First, it is heady and theological, not heart-warming and emotional. John doesn't give us the picture of Christmas we all love (sheep, donkeys, shepherds, Magi, and a baby born in a barn); he gives us a cosmic image of Jesus being more than just a sweet baby (which is easy for us to accept). John is trying to tell us in a poem that this Jesus is the Word, the Light, and the Life, and that he has existed since before creation. Jesus is God, and you can't separate the two from each other.

For us to come to grips with this passage (and a weak grip at that), we need to understand what is meant by "the Word." The Greek word used here is *logos*, which can mean several things. It can mean "word," or what we speak. It can also mean "reason" or "logic," the way we arrive at sound judgment. *Logos* can also mean conversation, an intimate dialogue between two people. So when John writes, "In the beginning was the Word," he is weaving one word into the fabric of this verse that means many different things, all of which are true of Christ. Those meanings are word, wisdom, and dialogue. And with that weaving, he also incorporates one of the most essential passages of Scripture, the opening of Genesis. With the phrase "in the beginning," John is purposefully reminding us of creation both here and in other places throughout his Gospel. That is how he relates Jesus as the Son of God. In Genesis 1, God speaks all of creation into being. "And God said" is the refrain we see over and over. Jesus as the Word is the action that establishes not only the first creation but also the second creation—the restoration of all creation.

Here's one other thing that is very critical. In Genesis, the climax of the creation saga is God creating humans. It's us—you and me—being created in God's own image. "So God created humankind in his image, in the image of God he created them" (Gen. 1:27). In John's prologue, the climax is the same image but reversed. "And the Word became flesh and lived among us" (John 1:14). God became a man. In his great Christmas hymn, Charles Wesley sums up the Incarnation in seven words: "Pleased as man with man to dwell."[1] In order for Christ to redeem the world, God had to become like us. He had to take on flesh and blood. Sometimes we say things like this: "I've walked in your shoes" or "I wish I could help you because I have been there before." God the Son does exactly that same thing! As Paul says in Philippians, Jesus, "being in the form of God, thought it not robbery to be equal with God: But made himself of no reputation, and took upon him the form of a servant, and was made in the likeness of men: And being found in fashion as a man, he humbled himself" (Phil. 2:6–8 KJV). My favorite Christmas poem by Thomas Philipot says it this way: "And God who man's frail house of earth composed / Himself in a frail house of earth enclosed."[2] Instead of us simply

---

1. "Hark! the Herald Angels Sing," *Hymnal.net*, https://www.hymnal.net/en/hymn/h/84.
2. Thomas Philipot, quoted in The Very Reverend John Hall, "Christmas Day Sermon, 2010," Westminster Abbey.

being made in God's image, God the Son made himself the perfect image of us—the image of the men and women we should all be.

And what did Christ the incarnate, the perfect God and perfect man do? John says he has given us grace upon grace, or as another translation puts it, gift upon gift. God among us and dwelling among us bestows on us the gift of becoming like him and moving us closer to the heart of the Father by becoming children of God.

Baptism is rich with imagery, but one of the last acts, which sometimes goes unnoticed, is when the family and godparents are given a candle, a light. The Word that we celebrate being born into the world is the same Word that was spoken at the commencement of creation: "Let there be light" (Gen. 1:3). The life of Jesus, the life of this Logos is the light that guides us, warms us, and allows us to see the world through his eyes. Is it any wonder that the first day of creation started with light? Throughout John's Gospel, the play between light and darkness is evident. Nicodemus comes to visit Jesus when it is night. Why? Nicodemus was searching for the Light!

The light is how we recognize Christ, but when God came to his own, we did not know him. Sometimes, we love darkness to our detriment. John 13:30 is perhaps the most chilling verse in all of Scripture: "After receiving the piece of bread, he [Judas] immediately went out. And it was night." Other times, we are so blinded by the darkness that we fail to see the light. We are like Mary Magdalene who, "early on the first day of the week, while it was still dark" (John 20:1), failed to recognize the resurrected Jesus and confused him with a gardener. She couldn't see Jesus for who he was. He is the true light that enlightens everyone.

What John is trying to tell us is that he who came into the world was also he who created the world. God was among us.

And in coming to us, living his life, dying on the cross, *and* being resurrected, Christ has come to restore all of creation, become the second Adam for us all, and give us grace upon grace. Don't get lost in the translation of this passage or fear what you don't understand—relish in it.

When you or I speak a word to one another, we create a situation, such as when we make a promise or even call someone by their name. Breath comes out of our lungs, thoughts come out of our minds, and our lips and tongues make the necessary shapes for us to utter the words we wish to express. Those words are part of us and part of our essence, and once spoken, they're hard to take back. The same is true for God. Most of us have sung one of my favorite Christmas hymns, "Of the Father's Love Begotten." The original opening phrase of this hymn in Latin is *Corde natus ex parentis.* There is a better translation that catches this opening phrase and makes God slightly more vulnerable: "Of the Father's heart begotten." Yes, Jesus was born of love, but God the Son came forth out of the heart of the Father. It is the mystery of the Trinity before us. This is God speaking in and through creation. This is God sharing the most intimate part of himself. This is the same God who speaks all things into being, who gave his only begotten Son, who spoke then, who speaks now, and who will continue to speak. And what does God speak? What does he say? God says light. God says life. God says love.

"In the beginning God created the heaven and the earth" (Gen. 1:1 KJV).

"In the beginning was the Word" (John 1:1).

"Then God said, 'Let there be light'" (Gen. 1:3).

A Lifelong Apprenticeship

John 1:29–42

In the Name of the Father, and of the Son, and of the
Holy Spirit. Amen.

See if this situation sounds familiar. You're having a perfectly normal conversation with someone, perhaps someone you don't know very well. Suddenly, you've lost track of the conversation, not because you weren't paying attention but because their response was completely random.

Here's an example. "Hi, Tom! How are you doing today?"

"Just fine, Bill. It is so nice of you to ask. How is everything with you?"

"Oh splendid, Tom. I just got that promotion at work I was wanting."

"Really? The one-cup system eliminates concerns about the cleanliness of traditional guest room coffee pots."

Bill is probably wondering if Tom has absolutely cracked or if he is using a Bluetooth connection to his mobile phone and is actually talking to someone else. Conversations that go a little awry like this are usually called *non sequitur* conversations. They don't follow logic very well and sometimes even leave us puzzled and wondering if we've missed something crucial and important. Or perhaps it is part of a larger joke or riddle, like asking someone to name two days of the week that start with the letter T and receiving an answer of today and tomorrow rather than Tuesday and Thursday. Sometimes the answer is true, but it's not necessarily the answer we were looking for.

Our Gospel passage has one of these conversations, and at face value it appears to show Jesus and two disciples talking past each other. Here's the scene: just before our reading in John 1, John the Baptist was at the River Jordan baptizing people with a baptism of repentance. As a result, some priests and Levites came to the river and asked if he is the Messiah, Elijah, or the Prophet. John the Baptist refuted this idea, explaining that he is the herald, the one coming before him whose sandals he is not worthy to untie. The next day is where our passage picks up, and it gets a little messy. John the Baptist declares that Jesus is the Lamb of God who takes away the sins of the world, but he also says he didn't recognize him as the Lamb or the Messiah until after he baptized him. On the third day of this story, Jesus appears again near the river, and John, for the second time, declares that Jesus is the Lamb of God. Two of John's disciples hear this, leave John the Baptist, and begin following Jesus. We can only imagine that they walk some distance before Jesus notices them following him and asks them a perfectly sensible question: "What are you looking for?" (John 1:38).

This is where the conversation takes an unexpected turn. First, most devout Jews living in first-century Palestine would have been hoping and praying for a coming Messiah, a king who would rout out the forces of Rome and liberate their country. Second, their own teacher, John the Baptist, had just identified Jesus as the Lamb of God, and we can assume that John had been teaching them his interpretation of the Scriptures. So they could have been searching for the new Prophet who baptizes with the Holy Spirit. Third, disciples typically did not just get up and leave their teacher. The bonds between teacher and disciple were very strong, so much so that most disciples lived with their teacher. Think about an apprentice of the ancient world who worked, crafted, and studied with the master of their craft, trying to mimic them.

The disciples answer Jesus with a question: "Rabbi, where are you staying?" (John 1:38). What we might consider a *non sequitur* is actually a very telling line. These disciples of John the Baptist are trying to tell Jesus they now want to be his disciples and do everything that being a disciple requires. And Jesus responds the way any teacher should: "Come and see" (John 1:39). He was perfectly open, perfectly welcoming.

By asking where Jesus was staying and indicating they want to be his disciples, they are asking less about the house he is in and more about where he is *dwelling*, where Jesus is *abiding*. True disciples want to abide and dwell with their teacher, their master. Only by being close to the master can the apprentice learn all about the trade and craft. Only by being close can they see the long hours, the problems encountered, and the solutions discovered, and begin to learn, copy, and understand. Being close to the master becomes not only a learning opportunity but also a blessing. In the world of trade guilds and handmade fabrications, the master agreed not only to teach but also to take his followers in and let them live with him. And because the wages were very low, he fed and clothed them until their apprenticeship was complete.

Many times, it was the master who decided if he could take on an apprentice or even how many he could take on at one time. Jesus's response is a welcoming invitation to those two men to come and, if they were stirred, to remain. My suspicion is that they already knew. Having been taught by John the Baptist, Andrew, one of the disciples, first goes and finds his brother Simon, later known as Peter, and brings him along. Andrew had been John's disciple, but John had accomplished his task of pointing to the Savior, handing off his disciples to Jesus to complete their learning and their training.

Disciples follow their master and do what their master does. As we read through the Gospels, we see that these disciples are constantly learning, often getting the craft of Kingdom-building wrong but striving for the day when they have mastered the task. Of course, they fail many times. There is a power play among James, John, and the rest of the disciples. Peter constantly asks the wrong questions and eventually denies knowing Jesus. Thomas, who had been one of the stalwarts, questions his faith because he didn't see the resurrected Jesus. Judas betrays Jesus, leading to his crucifixion. Still, Jesus never condemns any of his disciples for their failings. Rather, like a potter whose student can't get the form on the wheel right, Jesus takes them, gives them another example, and watches them continue to grow.

We call ourselves Christians—followers of Christ. A better term is *disciples* or, better yet, *apprentices*. We seek to be close to our Master. We want to learn to be more like Jesus. We abide with Jesus so we, like apprentices learning a trade, can learn all there is to know about how to be more like him. Jesus in turn promises to teach us, care for us, and feed us. Our yearning as Christians is then to pattern and model our lives directly after Christ, like an artist who copies a great painting so he can learn the techniques used to create the brush strokes. How do we do that?

Previously I mentioned *Being Christian*, the small book written by Rowan Williams, the former Archbishop of Canterbury. In it he explains four ways we exhibit our Christianity: baptism, Bible, Eucharist, and prayer. These are the tools we have and use during our training.

Let's dig a little more into what Archbishop Williams wrote. Baptism is where we start, where we take our first steps and see what the calling of being a Christian is all about. It is where we become part of the community. Being a Christian without community is impossible. It is where we learn to start being like Jesus and go where Jesus went. And where did he go? He went to a dark, fallen world, and he invites us also to journey with him to the darkest places in our world, proclaiming the same message and good news.

How do we know what to do? That's where the Bible becomes the tool of our trade. We as Christians expect God to speak to us, and we hear God's voice through the Bible. It is this tool that we all use to learn the craft and trade. It is full of surprises and turns we never expect at first glance, and that is what keeps us rooted in belief and purpose. When we have questions, we turn first to the sacred Scriptures and then to the scholars and theologians. The Scriptures are law, history, poetry, philosophy, prophecy, and letters—a library ready for the reader.

And when we grow weary, when our souls ache, and when we need bread for the journey, we come together for Eucharist, our meal with Christ and our fellow believers, united in time and space. Sometimes we call it communion because even when we don't feel pious and holy, even when we fail, Jesus Christ still tells us he wants our company. Communion is not some great reward for the holy. Communion exists because we are doing badly and need a cure, because we are not full but are still hungry and need to receive his body. We as the church are the body of Christ, and we receive the body of Christ so we may go out into this world *as* the body of Christ. Eucharist is what makes that possible.

And finally, there is prayer—our contemplation and resting in God. It is a time for us to grow in our own humanity so we can become godlike in a human way. Prayer is that moment when God who seems so far away can be as close as the next breath we take. Prayer is where we surrender our accomplishments and our failures, asking that in spite of ourselves and our efforts, God's will be done. In our prayers we also ask God to forgive us of our sins and failings, but we also pray that we are forgiven in the same measure that we forgive. When we pray our Lord's Prayer, we petition God to forgive "as we also have forgiven our debtors" (Matt. 6:12). It is that intimate time with the Master when our vision is clarified, our actions are disciplined, and the divine life slowly transforms us.

Do you see? Do you understand why we must have these four tools to be good disciples? However, don't forget the chief tool that drapes over us, that all we do must be grounded in love—our love of God, our love for our neighbors, and our love for our own selves.

While we live this earthly life, we will always be apprentices—there is always one more lesson for us to learn and one more failing for us to correct. Let us be good apprentices. Let us continue to dwell and abide with our Master and our Friend. And when we pattern our lives after the Master, people will not see us working in the world; they will see God active in the world. They will "come and see" when we are the body of Christ in the world. One of the prayers we say reminds us of our task as disciples: "Grant that your people, illumined by your Word and Sacraments may shine with the radiance of Christ's glory, that he may be known."[1] May we shine with the radiance of Christ's glory that he may be known.

---

1. *Book of Common Prayer*, 1979, 215.

The Logic of the Cross

1 Corinthians 1:10–18

In the Name of the Father, and of the Son, and of the
Holy Spirit. Amen.

L et's consider three vignettes. The first vignette is a small
rural town in South Texas that recently voted on a bond.
The bond proposed building a new elementary school
that would serve children in the fourth, fifth, and sixth grades,
and the price tag was just over $15 million. People wrote letters
to the editors, taking one of two sides. One side explained how
the school was necessary because of the aging buildings and
the lack of adequate wiring for technology, arguing that the
deferred maintenance would save the school district money in
the next decade. The opposition voiced their displeasure that the
bond would increase the tax rate and disproportionally affect

lower income families. They cited the school district's lack of responsibility in the upkeep of the current buildings and pointed out that teachers across the district needed raises rather than a new campus. Political signs went up around town, and on voting day, the opposition party won by 12 votes.

The next vignette is a young couple who met each other where they both worked, fell madly in love, and got married within six months. Each knew that the other was an avid fan of their respective alma maters, but neither understood the deeply held passions their partner had for their college football team. Each knew that their two universities would be playing each other in mid-November, but neither counted on the game of one-upmanship that would ensue. The husband put burnt orange and white lights on the house. The wife dyed the lawn maroon. The husband scrawled in big letters on his wife's car, "I love UT," and in response, the wife wrote "Longhorns are losers" on his truck. By the time the game was held weeks later, they couldn't even stand to watch it together, and each went to their separate friends' houses to watch the game. It was truly a house divided.

And in our final vignette, a company was hemorrhaging money. At the rate they were losing income, by the end of the year they would have to shutter the doors and sell the building. The quarterly directors' meeting was tense, and blame was placed everywhere. One member who thought he knew the answer offered this suggestion: "Obviously, we need to shift to a skeleton crew and only be open from 10:00 in the morning until 4:00 in the afternoon." Worried about what laying off most of their 50 employees would mean, the manager responded, "But customer service will suffer greatly. I've been thinking about trying some new items and running a newspaper ad to remind people we are here." Another person barked back about the waste of money, while still a fourth person wanted to make an announcement that the company was closing at the end of the month and to take their investments and run. There were yelling, name-calling, and tears. But no solution was found, mainly because everyone already believed they were right and the other people were wrong. The only thing they agreed on was tabling everything, meeting next week, and seeing if they could all think of different and better solutions by then.

All of us have been in situations where communal life has been strained. And if most churches are honest, they will admit that every church has probably had moment of dissension or controversy, be it a bad financial year, a scandal, or even an unpopular priest or minister. Disagreements and factions just seem to be part of life and what we deal with regularly. From family life to national life to church life, we all probably know of at least one example of people having an argument and getting wounded and hurt, and the relationships becoming so decimated that there is little chance for recovery. That's basically what Paul is addressing with the church at Corinth.

Corinth was a Greek city that had been a major metropolitan center for several hundred years. As such, the city had a diverse population: Greeks, Jews, traders from North Africa, and probably people from different parts of modern-day Turkey and Europe. And of course, Romans also lived there since Greece was then under the rule of the Roman Empire. As with any coastal city of the day, Corinth had a great number of visitors, many who probably were not Greeks. Paul visited the city and probably founded the church in Corinth—mostly likely a house church where people gathered in someone's home. Later in his letter, Paul describes various practices the Corinthians were engaged in that he found disconcerting. We get hints of this in the opening of 1 Corinthians.

Given the fact that Corinth was a melting pot, one of the issues Paul addresses in this letter is the divisions that are taking place in the church. In a multiethnic, multireligious, and multisocioeconomic city, the church in Corinth was beginning to reflect the cosmopolitan nature of that city. As a result, minor divisions were beginning to fester and grow. Word of the problems had gotten back to Paul, so he sent this letter as both a reminder and a warning. Because of these divisions, the church had started to lose sight of its real purpose. Rather than coming together as a community, the church was breaking into factions, and some of those divisions were coming from teachers or people who had come through the area. Among them was Cephas, whom we know as Peter. The division was literally tearing the community apart, and it is so distressing that people are reaching out to Paul to complain.

Paul is trying to get the focus back on the main thing—the cross—and that is probably the message he preached during his time in Corinth. The message of the cross is the paradox we all find ourselves in, and to the wise, it is foolishness. But the word Paul actually uses here is not *message*, but rather *logic*. For a culture steeped in Greek philosophy and culture, how does that all weigh when placed against the logic of Plato and Socrates, among others?

First, Paul appeals to the church to be of one purpose and not give in to factions and clichés that truly do not matter. There is no room for the cult of personality in the church. But this appeal is not a command because unity cannot be commanded. We can pray for it and discern how best to achieve it, but we cannot force or legislate unity. My own church, the Episcopal Church USA, is in the middle of a battle over unity. Without getting into all the problems and issues (there are several), part of the overarching question is not only how we remain the Episcopal Church but also how we continue in fellowship and unity with the rest of the Anglican Communion.

It all comes back to the cross. One way to think about an image of the cross is that we live out life founded on the logic of Jesus, following the pattern of his life. All of us as individuals and we as the church corporate must constantly check ourselves against what is true and what we think is true. One nineteenth-century Anglican priest called this living the "cruciformed" life—a life that is defined by self-sacrifice, bearing the burdens of others, not as a debased form of self-denial but as a life full of joy and thanksgiving. The logic is that the cross, this instrument of death, is the way to life, and the cross is life-affirming. When we focus on the cross and its message, we point not only ourselves but also those around us who do not know or understand to the love of God. When we take up our crosses, when we do the things we know we should be doing as the church, we literally transform the world.

But there is also a danger. Don't make Christ a cause. When we do that, we obscure the cross. Christ is not a cause; Christ is our motive. Because of his great love, because we have been forgiven for things we have done and left undone, we are propelled forward into the service of our Lord, and our motives are rendered true, good, and pure. Everything else only gets in the way and clouds the cross.

One of the painful truths we as Christians face (and this is true for Christians of all denominations) is declining membership or people not being active and engaged in the life of the community. There are thousands of theories as to why. Books, conferences, and guru speakers all address some of the issues, from societal evolution to problems with the Enlightenment, the advent of science, and interest in more Eastern and mystical religions. Some of that may very well be true. But the church must also be honest with itself; we have been fighting with each other for nearly 2,000 years. The Episcopal Church is embroiled in lawsuits over property. The Roman Catholic Church has been exposed for protecting priests they knew where committing heinous acts, and it will take a generation or two for people to trust the church again—if they ever do. We have had holy wars and crusades, and Christians have burned other Christians at the stake. All of this has been done in the name of Jesus—and it completely obscures the cross. No wonder so many people are dubious when it comes to trusting the institution that is the church.

So, my friends, go find the cross you must bear today. Don't obscure it. The message and logic of the cross may seem foolish to the world outside, but we know the power that the love of God provides. Let us all strive to be the church that Paul appeals for us to be and not get distracted by all the ancillary things. Let us keep Christ as our motive and the cross as our guide.

Choose Life

Deuteronomy 30:15–20

In the Name of the Father, and of the Son, and of the
Holy Spirit. Amen.

There are some points in history that are defined by a leader's speech or address. Some of those speeches make it into the annals of history and are taught still to this day. Sometimes, with the aid of historians, these addresses help us understand the time period or circumstances of the people who lived at that time. Many are known for only one or two quintessential phrases. For example, when President Abraham Lincoln wrote his "Gettysburg Address," he was not proclaiming a victory for the North but was mourning the deaths of a terrible battle, using it as a call to reclaim the freedom in the Republic of the United States: "Four score and seven years ago our fathers

. . ."[1] During the Second World War, Prime Minister Winston Churchill took to the radio and attempted to rally the British people after the fall of France, delivering his epic address that asked the British to fight on beaches and landing places so that in a thousand years people around the globe would say, "This was their finest hour."[2] Not all that long ago in Washington, DC, a Black Baptist minister who became both a prophet and a martyr gave an iconic cry for justice. Martin Luther King Jr. had a dream of equality and respect for others so that every person in the land could shout out, "Free at last! Free at last! Thank God Almighty, we are free at last!"[3]

These speeches define their eras. It is almost as if time hinges on them, and after those speeches, the world was never the same. This is very much what we find in our passage in Deuteronomy 30. Moses is giving his farewell address after being the leader of the children of Israel for about 40 years. He had been God's right-hand man, and because of God working through Moses, the Israelites had been brought out of Egypt and out of slavery. Moses had led the Hebrew children through the Red Sea and onto dry land, and when Moses cried to God for food, manna fell from heaven and quail were in the camp. Moses had led battles, and he had ascended Mount Sinai and brought the Ten Commandments down from God to the people. Moses had not just been their leader; he had been God's spokesman and the people's advocate

---

1. "The Gettysburg Address," *Abraham Lincoln Online*, http://www. abrahamlincolnonline.org/lincoln/speeches/gettysburg.htm.
2. "Their Finest Hour," *International Churchill Society*, https:// winstonchurchill.org/resources/speeches/1940-the-finest-hour/their-finest-hour/.
3. "'I Have a Dream' Speech," *History*, https://www.history.com/topics/ civil-rights-movement/i-have-a-dream-speech.

before God. And now Moses must say goodbye as the Israelites begin the next phase of their life as a nation. They are moving into the Promised Land, but Moses is not going with them. This is Moses's last will and testament, and what does he tell them? Choose life!

To our ears, this seems like a simple task, but we are missing both the context of the bulk of the Torah and the experience of living in this community and having Moses as a leader. Early on the Israelites' journey, God gave this newly formed nation a set of laws and codes. Most of them are found in the first five books of the Bible, known to us today as the Torah. Beginning with the Ten Commandments, God outlined what it means to look like a people called by God. The word we sometimes use for this is *sanctified*, or *sanctification*, and the simple definition is this: Israel is separated to be holy, called by God to be set apart from everyone else. The method of being holy rests in part on living the way God commanded Israel to live. Here are a few examples.

Exodus 23:19 prohibits boiling a small goat, a kid, in its mother's milk. Why is that a problem? First, think about the horrific image of milking a goat and then using the milk, which the kid had used to sustain its life, to cook it in. Second, it disturbs the parent-child relationship since the mother is providing the very thing her own offspring will be cooked in. Third, it is recorded as a practice of the pagans who inhabited the Promised Land. So in order to be set apart, God told them not to boil a kid in its mother's milk.

What about the harvesting of grain and crops?

> *When you reap the harvest of your land, you shall not reap to the very edges of your field, or gather the gleanings of your harvest. You shall not strip your*

*vineyard bare, or gather the fallen grapes of your
vineyard; you shall leave them for the poor and the
alien: I am the LORD your God.*

—Lev. 19:9–10

Why leave some of your harvest in the field? Because, the poor, the traveler, the immigrant, and the widow might need that food in order to survive. And if you are a sanctified nation, you must care for these people since no one else will.

Here's a good one, also from Leviticus: "You shall not render an unjust judgment; you shall not be partial to the poor or defer to the great: with justice you shall judge your neighbor" (Lev. 19:15). I don't know about you, but for me, that one begins to hit a little closer to home. We could all say, "But I thought we were supposed to be kind to the poor and punish the rich. I thought justice was meting out what people deserve because of their status." When you start dealing in socioeconomic judgments, you pervert justice— you miscarry or mishandle justice. And since God judges by the heart instead of status or wealth, we also should render justice by the heart.

I hope you see how the Law was and is life-giving. Just as we have laws that protect us and render situations equitable (and some laws we dread, such as paying our taxes on April 15), God's Law was there to give order to society. But most importantly, God gave Israel the Torah to make them a blessing to all nations. Go back and read our psalm for today: "Happy are they whose way is blameless, who walk in the law of the LORD" (Ps. 119:1). When you can, find about 15 minutes or so this week, read through Psalm 119, which extols the virtues of the Torah. It is from that psalm that we get the well-known verse, "Thy word [i.e., Torah] is a lamp unto my feet, and a light unto my path" (Ps. 119:105 KJV).

Fast-forward about 1,400 years to first-century Palestine, and another teacher is talking about the Law. When we read through the Gospels, we hear Jesus tell his listeners that he came to fulfill the Law, the Torah, and not to abolish it. He then makes the Torah even more demanding in several cases. For example, you don't have to kill someone to incur judgment upon yourself; you only have to be angry with them, and you will be judged. Jesus is actually demanding his followers to hold themselves not only to the Law but to a standard more stringent than the Law. I have heard Christians say many times that because of Jesus's death and resurrection, we don't have to do all that stuff the Jews did. Well, yes, we don't have to go to the temple and make sacrifices, but no as well. The fact that Jesus fulfilled the Law doesn't mean we can ignore the Law; it means we have a higher calling than the Law.

How does the Law give life? First, the Law calls us to look to the needs of others—our family, our neighbors, and all those we encounter. Second, the Law points to justice and what is right and fair. Third, the Law points us to God since it separates us from all the other religions or idols of our life. Moses says in his farewell speech to choose life, a pleading call to continue walking in the way of the Torah. Choose life that you might live a fulfilled life, a life pleasing to God, a sanctified life.

How do we do that today as Christians? First, we need to deny those things that are not life-affirming, those things that bring death to our souls and our bodies. Take for instance the seven deadly sins: pride, wrath, envy, greed, gluttony, lust, and sloth. Most of our sins, even the little ones, fall into one of these categories. Some are rather self-explanatory, but what about gluttony? Does gluttony concern only our stomachs, or can gluttony also mean having just a little bit too much to drink last night or lacking discipline when it comes to fasting days such as Ash Wednesday?

What about pride? Is it just the politicians or athletes on television who are proud and boastful? Or does pride also mean our lack of faith in God and believing that God only helps those who help themselves? Does pride also lead to racism or snobbery over our family name? One of the reasons these sins are deadly is that they are like taking small doses of poison that eventually will kill you. They usually start with a small, insignificant remark or gesture, or even just a passing thought.

So then, what about life? What is life-giving? What would the Torah, Moses, and Jesus say we ought to do to in fact choose life? Perhaps consider some of these. Enjoy simpler things. Be patient with yourself as you strive to do good. Celebrate the love of your spouse, your parents, and your children. Turn off the television, and spend time with people you care about. Help the struggling mother with her groceries. Forgive someone, especially if they don't deserve it. Worship God with all your heart, mind, soul, and strength. Visit someone in prison. Clothe the naked. Give rest to the weary. Love your neighbor as yourself. Love yourself the way God loves you.

"See, I have set before you today life and prosperity, death and adversity. . . . Choose life" (Deut. 30:15, 19).

Trapped in the Dark

John 3:1–17

*In the Name of the Father, and of the Son, and of the
Holy Spirit. Amen.*

The two friends had been in the car all day long. Day had turned into night several hours before, and they were both ready to get to their homes and get some sleep. Earlier, while still a good distance away from a critical turnoff, they had formulated a plan. The person driving would drive to his house and unload his luggage, and then the person who owned the truck would go on to his home. They lived about 20 miles apart, so one wrong turn would make the difference in about an hour's drive for the two of them.

The passenger was on his phone, chatting away with someone about nothing too important. As the turn approached, the driver turned on his signal and started changing lanes, ready to exit onto the smaller highway. The passenger, somewhat startled by the change in course, blurted out, "No! Not this exit! What are you doing?" Even though the driver knew he was about to make the turn necessary to save time, he quickly moved the car back to the interstate. The passenger continued talking on the phone for a good while, and once he hung up, he asked, "What were you thinking? That's not the way home!" The driver, trying not to upset the situation, quietly said, "That was the way to *my* home, not yours."

Our Gospel passage this morning introduces us to Nicodemus. He is a Pharisee, which means he is not only a leader in the Jewish community but also extremely well versed in the Torah and the Hebrew Scriptures. He is one of the people who sits with, prays with, and studies the Law, making note of every jot and tittle. Compared to anyone else, Nicodemus is an expert. He knows his Bible, and more than likely, people come to him with questions. And now, during the night, Nicodemus comes to Jesus with some questions because he is in the dark.

Why at night? In another story in the next chapter (John 4), we encounter someone else Jesus has a dialogue with, the woman at the well—a Samaritan woman, no less. Jesus also engages with this woman, but it is at high noon, the brightest part of the day. We can begin to make an exegetical assumption about John's Gospel. There is the interplay between light and darkness, or John critiquing the Pharisees. There are even defined roles— Nicodemus couldn't be seen with Jesus because of his position and power (much like the Prophet Jeremiah being visited by King Zedekiah in prison) and the woman who needed to go about her daily task of drawing water from a well. But I think all these miss the crucial point.

Sometimes, especially when we know (or at least think we know) something, it turns out not to be the case. And more often than not, it is the darkness that is the proving ground as well as the teacher. How many of us have gone to our kitchens in the middle of the night, leaving the light off because we know our way, only to stub our toe on a chair, step on a shoe, or grope around looking for a light switch? We know the way, but we can't see it; we can only feel it out. Or after a disastrous storm when the streetlights are out and houses are damaged how many times have we heard people who are interviewed say it took them a while to find their house because all the familiar landmarks were gone? Some of us have dealt with deep personal struggles and issues—our very own dark nights of the soul. What have we learned? Did we learn anything at all? Were we open to learning or just terrified by what we thought we might encounter?

We use darkness as a metaphor for not only *not* seeing what is in front of us but also not seeing what we should see. Or we use the darkness to fool ourselves into distrusting those we *should* trust, much like the two friends in the car trying to get home.

Jesus is seeking to help Nicodemus see what he already knows in a new way. If Jesus is the light we hear about in the prologue to this Gospel, then he is trying to guide Nicodemus through the dark, helping him not to trip up on his own questions, doubts, and misunderstandings. Using imagery such as water and the Spirit, along with a story about Moses that would be familiar to a teacher of the Torah, Jesus essentially says, "This is the point, don't you see?" Nicodemus is not in the dark because he failed a Torah class or missed a few questions on his General Ordination Exams, Pharisee edition. He is in the dark about the revelation of who the Son of Man is, which would mean a completely different mindset, a completely different approach to God, and a complete surrendering of his former understanding, his former self. He must be born anew, born from above.

In her book *Learning to Walk in the Dark*, Barbara Brown Taylor recounts a trip she took with two friends into a cave. One of the things she noticed was that darkness can produce its own beauty. Sitting in a portion of the cave that no natural light had ever illuminated, Taylor recalls being able to faintly make out tiny, shiny objects. She explains it this way:

> *When I reach up to turn off my lamp, I see something impossibly sparkly just above my head, and I stand up to get a better look. It is a long thin fissure in the rock that is full of tiny crystals, and every one of them catching the light and tossing it back and forth. . . . I aim my headlamp at some pieces that have broken off, choose the one with the most glitter in it, and put it in my backpack before turning off the lamp and sitting down in the dark.* [1]

A little while later, after she returned to the house she was staying in, Taylor makes this discovery:

> *Back in my room that night, I unpack my backpack, surprised to find the stone at the bottom. Remembering how it glittered in the darkest part of the cave, I hold it under the reading lamp anticipating miniature fireworks. Instead, it looks like a piece of road gravel. . . . If I tossed it in my driveway, no one would even lean down to pick it up. What in the world made me think this was a precious stone?*

---

1. Barbara Brown Taylor, *Learning to Walk in the Dark* (New York: Harper-Collins, 2014), 127.

But the stone is not the problem. The light is the problem. Even the reading light is too much. Rummaging in my pack for a penlight, I click it on and aim the beam at my hand. The stone turns into a diamond factory before my eyes, fully as dazzling as I remember. If I were small enough to walk into the opening in this rock, I would walk on a crystal carpet with a crystal ceiling above my head.[2]

Taylor went looking for beauty *in the dark*. Nicodemus comes looking for answers *in the dark*. Taylor later discovered that what might be humdrum and ordinary, or even the cause of great angst in our life, what she calls "full-solar Christianity," can shine, sparkle, and be immensely beautiful, but only *in the dark*.

Jesus and Nicodemus talk at cross-purposes because Nicodemus can't yet see what the beauty of Christ's message in the dark is really saying. Nicodemus wants everything he knows to be explained in one instant—one moment in time—like turning on the floodlights on a stage. He even gives Jesus his starting point, "Rabbi, we know that you are a teacher" (John 1:2). We know!

How often are we Nicodemus? How often do we cease to be startled and mesmerized by the Scriptures, by our Liturgy, or even by God because "we know"? We accumulate knowledge, and sometimes that knowledge acts as a straitjacket to faith rather than a microscope that zooms into our life or a telescope that gazes into the heavens to see the mystery of creation beyond ourselves. Nicodemus, mystified by what he has heard, asks a question I think is also important for us ask, both as individuals and as the church. "How can anyone be born after having grown old?" (John 3:4).

---

2. Taylor, 130.

After growing old, we become set in our ways. After growing old, we claim a certain knowledge that only time and experience can impart. After growing old, we know all about God. After all, the quintessential verse of all Christian faith is right here in this very chapter: "For God so loved the world" (John 3:16). We have heard this since our youth, we have seen it on a placard at the Super Bowl, and we have worn it as a badge to distinguish between those who believe and those who are perishing.

Are we Nicodemus, already knowing the right answers, the good Sunday school answers, but trapped in the dark without seeing the beauty of crystalline rocks around us? Or is there a new insight and a born-again experience, being "born from above" (John 3:7) that we are being called to? "But to all who received him, who believed in his name, he gave power to become children of God" (John 1:12).

Nicodemus came to Jesus by night because he was searching for light. "The light shines in the darkness, and the darkness did not overcome it" (John 1:5).

The Unknown God

Acts 17:22–31

In the Name of the Father, and of the Son, and of the Holy Spirit. Amen.

Do any of you remember the artwork that adorned offices and classrooms in the 1990s? There was one style of picture I saw everywhere, the autostereogram. It is a two-dimensional image, usually with some sort of repeating pattern that when viewed at a divergent angle renders an illusion of a three-dimensional image. I remember one from high school that I saw almost daily for a year. It supposedly had the image of a fighter jet embedded in the patterns, but I could never see it. In fact, I have still never found the hidden image in any autostereogram I've come across, though I have tried everything from standing close to moving across the room to standing at odd angles, and even looking at it cross-eyed. Alas, I never see anything, and to this day when I encounter one of these images, I have to ask what I am supposed to be seeing.

In our passage in Acts, Paul is in Athens, a city known as a major center of learning. He has been strolling through the city waiting for Timothy and Silas to join him there. The book of Acts records that he became distressed about the city being full of idols and images of worship and affection to which the Greeks paid homage. Practicing Jews, as Paul had been his entire life, could not abide idols. Psalm 115 goes so far as to say that not only are idols the work of human hands but that those who fabricate them are spiritually dead.

> *Their idols are silver and gold, the work of human hands. They have mouths, but do not speak, eyes, but they do not see. They have ears, but do not hear; noses, but do not smell. . . . Those who make them are like them; so are all who trust in them.*
> —Ps. 115:4–6, 8

Of particular interest to Paul is one altar with this inscription: "To an Unknown God" (Acts 17:23). Using the opportunity presented to him, Paul decides to give an argument for who this unknown god is. First, he goes to the synagogue among people whose thinking is similar to his and then goes to the marketplace. We need to understand that these marketplaces, *agoras* as they were called, were public places, not just large farmers' markets. An agora was a gathering place where citizens of the city could debate political life and spiritual matters, display works of art, and even take part in athletic competitions. It was the literal heart and center of the city. Everyone, from rich to poor, slave to free, man or woman, would pass through this area, shopping or taking time to listen to whoever the speaker of the day might be. To use an image familiar to us, Paul is standing on the street corner of a busy intersection talking and debating with whoever crosses his path.

Our story picks up after some of the philosophers from the Epicurean and Stoic schools hear Paul in the agora and take him to Areopagus. It was not so much an arrest (like putting Paul on trial for what he had been saying) as it was akin to taking Paul to a university philosopher's club meeting and having him impart knowledge of ideas and teachings, both new and strange, to the hearers. It was a meeting of the minds—a meeting of debate—and sometimes there were verdicts on moral issues as a result of the debate and dialogue. So Paul, an apostle, a Jew-turned-Christian, and not a philosopher by their definition, is invited to address this group and explain this "new teaching" that "sounds rather strange" (Acts 17:19, 20).

One of the things to note about Paul's speech is that he meets the people in the Aeropagus as they are. He starts outlining and detailing what he has seen and observed. Calling them "extremely religious" (Acts 17:22), Paul uses what they already know as the crack in the door to step into their world. Something that is repulsive to Paul, the use and worship of idols, becomes the gateway for him to proclaim the gospel to these pantheistic pagans. Pointing out the altar dedicated to the unknown god, Paul seizes the opportunity to explain not only who God, the God of all creation, is from his perspective but also that these Athenians have already been worshiping this God even though he is unknown to them.

In Greek mythology, Zeus is the god of the sky and thunder, the king of all the other gods in the Pantheon and the chief god of men. While there were many other gods such as Poseidon, Apollo, and Hades, Zeus was one of the oldest, most revered, and most feared of the gods. In the second century BC, Aratus, a Greek poet, wrote a poem based on astronomy and climate as they understood it. This poem became revered among the Greeks and about a century later among the Romans. Cicero even translated it from Greek into Latin. For our purposes, what is so remarkable is that Paul quotes Aratus's poem even though it is an invocation to Zeus. In one of the verses, Aratus declares that through Zeus, all the gods and men of earth "live and move and have their being," and then harkens back to some of the early Greek myths that all men "too are his offspring." Paul appeals to his audience by using their own poems and teachings to reframe the argument that it is this unknown God—not Zeus, but the God of Abraham, Isaac, Jacob, and Jesus—who should be the object and devotion of all their worship. Paul wants the Athenians to see that they are already close and just need to take the final step. They are within grasp. Like the autostereogram, they just need to refine their focus.

One of the points important for us to remember is that Paul tells the Athenians to look around! It is possible to recognize and see God in all creation. We can marvel at many things we see each day and give due worship to God, but so much rests on us recognizing the work of God in creation.

One of the most remarkable canticles in the Liturgy for Morning Prayer is the *Benedicite*, the Song of Creation. This canticle comes from an addition to Daniel found in the Apocrypha, in the scene where the three young men are cast into the fiery furnace. This addition has the three men singing their song in the midst of the flames. It is a song that praises God through all the works of creation, from the cosmos to the earth and its plants and creatures, and finally to humans and the people of God. All creation reflects the Creator and sings praises to him forever and ever.

There is an amusing story about a little Anglican vicar in a not-so-noteworthy parish in nineteenth-century England who had a habit of walking around his village and countryside making up his own version of the *Benedicite*, including some of the creatures and people he saw daily. Perhaps he wandered around saying something like this: *O ye slug that eats our crops, praise him and magnify him forever. O ye rabbits that hop down the lane, praise him and magnify him forever. O ye blacksmith, who beats iron and metal into tools we can use, praise him and magnify him forever.*

In similar fashion, Christopher Smart, an eighteenth-century English poet, captured the same idea in his masterpiece "*Jubilate Agno*" ("Rejoice in the Lamb"). In the poem, Smart discusses his cat Jeoffry, and that his cat in his own way offers praises to God.

> For I will consider my Cat Jeoffry.
> For he is the servant of the Living God duly and daily serving him.
> For at the first glance of the glory of God in the East he worships in his way.
> For this is done by wreathing his body seven times round with elegant quickness.
> For then he leaps up to catch the musk, which is the blessing of God upon his prayer.[1]

We are called to look, search, and find where God is moving in our midst, where his creation extols the beauty and grandeur of the Maker—perhaps even in a sense an unknown Maker. This requires us to look with new eyes, to look at everything in a fresh, childlike way. And perhaps we should especially look for God in

---

1. Christopher Smart, "Jubilate Agno," *Poetry Foundation*, https://www.poetryfoundation.org/poems/45173/jubilate-agno.

the unlikely—the novel, the piece of art, the skill of athletes, the work of poetry, the lessons of a master teacher, the scientist who discovers an atom. Each is performed and created with such skill and facility as to beckon us to recall that in God alone we live and move and have our being.

But there is also a danger. We must not and cannot allow the creation to outshine the Creator. For all the beauty we see, for all the marvels of this age, we cannot lose sight of who all things point to. If we lose sight of that, other things become an idol. An idol doesn't have to be made of silver and gold or fashioned in the form of humans or animals. Idols can be anything, even something so small that it may seem insignificant. From wealth and social status to possessions or even religion itself, we all have idols we are tempted to follow. And we line them up over and against God, sometimes meaning well but ultimately allowing them to draw our attention away from Almighty God and focus instead on the finite creation of human skill.

Just as Paul strolled through Athens, we all need to take stock of the idols that have snuck into our lives. Let's discuss a few that I see often, sometimes even daily. The one that comes most readily to mind is God and country. Being patriotic, serving our country in the Armed Forces or as a public servant, and being a good citizen are all right and commendable. But when we as Christians align our interests with political policies rather than the interests of the Kingdom of heaven or treasure the cloth of the flag more than the wood of the cross, we turn our country into an idol.

A second idol that dominates our culture today is the entertainment industry. From sports and athletes to musicians and bands to movie franchises and actors, many of us fall victim to the prevalent cult of celebrity. We watch and follow our teams or leagues to a point of obsession and end up knowing, in many cases, the happenings and doings of the celebrities more than the neighbor down the street or the coworker we pass every day. We manage our schedules around kickoff times or become anxious if we miss one minute of our Wednesday night sitcom. We claim we have no time to read Scripture, be present for the Liturgy on Sunday, or even help the people in our neighborhood, but we can make time for things that do not matter in the grand scheme of things.

I have my own idols I must deal with, and many of them have started off as wonderful exercises or even noble causes. None of these examples are bad unto themselves, but it is what we make them. It is where we place them. You see, it is good and right to love things such as our country or a star golfer. We are to love all creation. But we are to love God supremely, not exclusively. If we loved God exclusively, then when would we love our neighbor or even ourselves? God calls us to love him supremely and to have no idols come before him.

So where are all our idols? Are they like the monuments and idols in Athens, dominating our view of the world and ourselves and rendering God to a corner, perhaps even with the label of the unknown God? Or are we putting our affections for all these worldly trappings in the right order?

Can These
Bones Live?

Ezekiel 37:1–14

*In the Name of the Father, and of the Son, and of the
Holy Spirit. Amen.*

One thing I think all of us can agree on is that we are living in precarious times. As I write this, there is a sense of anxiety, not about one issue but about a whole host of problems and fears. People around the globe are seeing their major financial markets crash, have suddenly found themselves unemployed, and are isolating themselves in their homes. In many places, people feel fear and frustration about one problem—a virus, COVID-19. We are struggling to keep our wits, our culture, and our way of life against an onslaught of an infection from something so small that it takes a microscope in a laboratory to see it. We are literally and actually attempting to ward off a disease we cannot see. That makes many of us afraid, worried about our bank accounts, and depressed because we are living essentially in exile.

Many of us know the story in our reading in Ezekiel. Israel was a nation that Moses led to the Promised Land. Over several generations, these people lived under judges who administered laws or under kings who brought both glory and shame to the nation. Eventually, Israel split into two countries, Israel in the north and Judah in the south. They lived as two separate nations until the overpowering Assyrians and Babylonians forced them into exile. These empires bound the Israelites' kings in chains, took their nobles and elites to live in their countries, and left a remnant of people behind. These least desirable people lived in ruined cities that had been smoldering for days or weeks. The Temple, the house where God's Name resided, was desecrated and destroyed. All hope was lost. They became a dead people. All that remained were the bones of a former nation, the bones of people who had been family and friends.

Using our mind's eye, let's put ourselves in Ezekiel's place. Picture your favorite place in the world—a spot in the mountains, a sandy beach, your yard, an open pasture filled with springtime flowers. Imagine that the place you love is now devoid of beauty, and all you see are bones. These are sun-bleached bones with no marrow or sign of life, only dry, brittle bones stacked on top of bones. Everything we love and cherish is in front of us, and it is dead. We lost our jobs—here are the bones of it. Our retirement account is depleted—its bones are over there. The business we took a lifetime to build—a heap of bones is all that is left. My child is a senior and was supposed to go to college, but now I can't afford to send her—here are the bones of that dream.

Then we hear a voice. "Jim, can these bones live? Sarah, can these bones live? Michael and Courtney, Jose and Karen, can these bones live?"

And we respond to the voice, either out of sorrow, fatigue, bewilderment, or sheer frustration, "O Lord GOD, you know" (Ezek. 37:3). Notice that Ezekiel never says yes, and he never says no. Like so many of us who pray our prayers, Ezekiel, in spite of his desperation, puts his trust in the knowledge that God *can* act, even when he is given only dead bones.

Think about the story of Lazarus being raised from the dead after four days. He wasn't just asleep, and he wasn't dead for just a few moments and then resuscitated. He had been dead long enough for a minor protest to arise because Jesus wanted the tomb opened. Why? Jesus was going to call to Lazarus. The same voice that asked Ezekiel if bones could live was now going to show that not only could a nation be reborn but you and I could be made whole. God created this world by speaking it into existence. He spoke to Ezekiel in a vision, and the valley of bones began to regenerate. Bone came to corresponding bone, and tissue, muscle, and flesh brought together something dead. Eventually, the breath of life was bestowed on a multitude.

And God the Son also summoned Lazarus—"Lazarus, come out!" (John 11:43), and he who was dead was brought back to life.

At times like these, I often reflect on a passage in Romans. Trying to assure the church in Rome, Paul asks them this question: "Who will separate us from the love of Christ? Will hardship, or distress, or persecution, or famine?" (Rom. 8:35). I imagine that if Paul were writing today, he would add, "Will war, or terrorists, or plague? Will the coronavirus and all the turmoil it has caused—will these separate us from the love of Christ?" He says no, "neither death, nor life . . . nor things present, nor things to come . . . nor anything else in all creation" (Rom. 8:38–39). Paul further explains that not one thing "will be able to separate us from the love of God in Christ Jesus our Lord" (Rom. 8:39). My friends, this is such great news—this is the essence of the very gospel itself.

God's love is ever enduring. God loved Israel, and that is why he gave such a profound vision to Ezekiel of hope, promise, and restoration to new life. Jesus loved Lazarus, even weeping over him, and that love is what called forth Lazarus from his tomb, still bound by his grave clothes. And God loves us still, especially in times of crisis, and neither death nor ruin—nothing—can separate us from the love of God.

During the season of Lent, many of us take a second look into our spiritual lives. Some of us keep a fast of some sort, while others take on daily tasks and obligations. We all take a little extra effort to ponder where we sin—where we miss the mark—and attempt to put our lives in right order. Sadly, during the COVID-19 crisis, most churches were not able to share the journey that Holy Week calls us to in preparation for Easter. But you see, Easter is all about new life—resurrected life. Perhaps if we can find just a hint of a silver lining in all this, it is that we were forced to reconsider ourselves and take stock in what we think is important and worth our energy. During the pandemic, we were forced to look after our neighbors and live through this ordeal, not as individuals but as a community bound together in love and hope. We were forced to live in exile.

But the body of Christ, the church, is perhaps strongest outside the doors of the church. That is when the real work of the church is done, when every phone call you make, every email you send, every prayer you say to encourage and uplift someone, and even every silly Facebook post of you singing a song exhibits your love for others. The work Jesus calls us to do is being done in new, challenging ways because we are loving our neighbors as ourselves. An empty church means we all have more to do where we are.

Things will soon return to normal yet will somehow be different. You see, a resurrected body is whole, but it is also somewhat different. Why do you think Mary Magdalene and the travelers on the road to Emmaus didn't recognize Jesus on Easter Day? Can you see how things might change but change for the better? Can you imagine and live into a dream of a restored creation, a restored reality? What does being a people coming out of exile mean? How should we then live?

Listen! Can you hear the bones rattling? "I will put my spirit within you, and you shall live" (Ezek. 37:14). New life is coming! And when the day comes, all of us will hear Jesus call out to us, "Lazarus, come out!" (John 11:43).

Who Better to
Serve Than Christ?

Romans 6:12–23

*In the Name of the Father, and of the Son, and of the
Holy Spirit. Amen.*

O ne activity that all of us engage in daily is making choices.
Some of these choices start rather early in our day. Do
I want coffee or tea? Which shirt should I wear? With
whom should I eat lunch today? Choices are part of our everyday
living. There are choices we must put great thought into such as
choosing a university to attend or deciding when to retire. And
there are choices we might make more subconsciously such as
which parking place we claim in the parking lot or which channel
we turn to when we watch the evening news.

Let me give you a warning, especially in light of issues in
this nation regarding civil rights, racism, and beliefs of men and

women during the early days of the settlement of this continent by Europeans. This is something we unfortunately gloss over in all our discussions about these issues. They are problems that exist in many parts of the world today and under many guises, some so despicable and heinous that I dare not even name them.

We are going to use the language of slavery since that is the language that Paul used. Slaves were common in the Roman Empire in the first century, so it was an image the recipients of Paul's letter to the church at Rome would have been familiar with, even if they were not someone's slave. Paul is not condoning slavery; he is using it as an image, a metaphor, and if it makes us uncomfortable, good. That is what he intends to do.

Whether we recognize it or not, whether we are cognizant of it or not, whether we acknowledge it or not, we are all slaves to something, even ideas, causes, or our own bad habits in life. We are slaves to routine and ritual. We are perhaps slaves to one political party or another. Some of us might be slaves to alcohol or drugs. Maybe food calls and beckons at odd hours. Perhaps we are slaves to greed, pride, and envy. We have things we know we are slaves to and things we don't realize we are slaves to until they are taken away from us.

The church has broken these down into seven categories: pride, greed, wrath, envy, lust, gluttony, and sloth. We call these the seven deadly sins. These aren't deadly in the sense that if you happen to be a little proud today you will spend eternity in some sort of everlasting damnation. No, what these seven sins are is the way we chip away at our humanity, at what God intended us to be. In doing so, we become slaves to sin—not slaves to the world, not slaves to ourselves, but slaves to sin. It is a slippery slope, like taking a small dose of poison every day or being on the event horizon of a black hole that is fast approaching. It is what holds us as human beings in the bondage of sin. The work of sin gives a payment, a wage, and "the wages of sin is death" (Rom. 6:23). Death becomes the ultimate end every time—no exception.

Let's pause for a moment and think about our choices. Think about the last 24 hours and the choices you made, both for the good and for the bad.

Consider these words of Moses: "See, I have set before you today life and prosperity, death and adversity. I call heaven and earth to witness against you today that I have set before you life and death, blessings and curses. Choose life so that you and your descendants may live, loving the LORD your God, obeying him, and holding fast to him" (Deut. 30:15, 19–20).

Consider the words of Jesus: "No one can serve two masters; for a slave will either hate the one and love the other, or be devoted to the one and despise the other" (Matt. 6:24).

Consider these words of Peter: "Even to them which stumble at the word, being disobedient: whereunto also they were appointed. But ye are a chosen generation, a royal priesthood, an holy nation . . . that ye should shew forth the praises of him who hath called you out of darkness into his marvellous light" (1 Pet. 2:8–9 KJV).

There are two choices all of us have to make. We who call ourselves Christians have been claimed as Christ's own, as slaves to righteousness for sanctification. We are no longer bound by sin *unless* we continue to choose that pattern of living. But that means our whole self or, as the Eucharistic Prayer in Rite I says, "We offer and present unto thee, O Lord, our selves, our soul *and* bodies, to be a reasonable, holy, and living sacrifice" (emphasis added).[1] The choice is not a one-time recognition and acknowledgment of our faith; it is the continual active, aware, and engaging discipleship

---

1. "Eucharistic Prayer 1," Rite I Service of the *Book of Common Prayer*, 336.

to Christ. It is our slavery—a reasonable, holy, and *living slavery*—devoted to Christ, devoted to God.

One of the great twentieth-century philosophers, the much lauded and Nobel Laureate Bob Dylan, once wrote, "You're gonna have to serve somebody, Well, it may be the devil or it may be the Lord, but you're gonna have to serve somebody."[2]

Moses, Paul, Peter, and Bob all have it right. You are a slave—a servant—to someone or something. Call it what you will—power, greed, supremacy, idols, politics, alcohol, celebrity worship, sex, Xbox, Facebook, fitness, food, and the list goes on and on—only you and God know what you are a slave to.

We as the church—not just your particular church, not just whatever diocese or convention your church is a member of, but the church universal—need to come to a reckoning and decide who we are slaves to. That is difficult work. It is not in our nature to become bonded as slaves to anyone, yet we do it all the time, even when we don't realize it. Are we slaves to doctrine? Perhaps we are slaves to denomination—I'm Episcopal, you're Baptist or Catholic, and am I thus better? Do we give in to the lie that all that matters is how much we love Jesus and that that is as far as our faith takes us and we refuse to live into that faith by thought, word, and deed? Or instead of using the Bible, our holy and sacred Scriptures as something to extol, to lift up, to heal the battered, to give hope to the myriads of people who need the Life it proclaims, do we use it as a weapon against others? Perhaps we twist the Bible to judge the poor because they must be lazy, or those of a different nationality so we must fear them, or those with a political ideology so far from ours that they must be wrong because the Bible says we are right.

---

2. Bob Dylan, "Gotta Serve Somebody," from the album *Slow Train Coming*, https://www.bobdylan.com/songs/gotta-serve-somebody/.

"We offer and present unto thee, O Lord, our selves, our souls and bodies."[3] If we are slaves to Jesus, it means we are left with the opportunity to serve him all the time, not just when we choose. It means we cannot turn our Christianity on and off at a whim. We can't be Christians today yet neglect our Christian duty the next six days. Look at George Herbert's words in his hymn "King of Glory, King of Peace": "Seven whole days, not one in seven, I will praise Thee."[4]

We can't make one decision as a Christian and another as a non-Christian or a humanist, claiming that the two problems are mutually exclusive. Every decision we make must work through the filter of what we profess to be the ultimate and only truth. We can't share the peace of the Lord at church while treating someone with utter contempt. We can't pray and beg for the forgiveness of our sins yet hold a decades-old grudge and demand satisfaction from those people who have hurt us.

If we are slaves, if we are servants of Christ, it must become who we are all the time. By practicing our faith, praying our faith (because praying shapes believing), and seeking ways to be the church *out there*—not just inside the church doors—we learn how to be disciples of God.

Who could we better serve than Christ? Who or what could be more life-giving than Christ himself? What could be more joyous than working alongside each other with the purposes of God as our task, the lifting up of all men and women as our call, and the knowledge that we do all these things because we love our God supremely?

---

3. "Eucharistic Prayer 1," Rite I Service of the *Book of Common Prayer*, 336.
4. George Herbert, "King of Glory, King of Peace," *Hymntime*, http://www.hymntime.com/tch/htm/k/g/l/o/kglokpea.htm.

Acknowledgments

Many tasks we engage in require the help of individuals who, even though it might not be their project, render aid that cannot be calculated. Sometimes, little things that seem like a small job provide help in ways that are incalculable. It might be changing a word or phrase here, encouragement to try a new and difficult writing technique there, or even the criticism that might sting when first rendered but it is something the writer or homilist needs to hear. There are a few people who saw almost all the sermons in this book in some draft form, and then there are others who read through the book with a red grading pen and marked up some of the sermons to the point I thought I was back in graduate school. To each of these individuals and communities of faith, I give my undying thanks and gratitude.

Many thanks to the now-Reverends Mikel Brightman, Dexter Lesieur, Karen Morris, Gerald Phelps, Arnoldo Romero, and Betsy Stephenson who comprised the first class of Iona Collaborative in the Diocese of West Texas and are all now bi-vocational priests serving in parishes and missions in our diocese. They listened to many of these sermons in their infant stages as we journeyed together for three years.

Thank you to Dr. Clark Hendley, the Reverend Nate Bostain, the Reverend Daniel Strandlund, the Reverend David Chalk, and the Venerable Mike Besson for being wonderful assigned and unassigned mentors. They read all these sermons with not only theological eyes but also with the ability to flesh out arguments that were weak or provide ideas that strengthened each of these sermons.

To the Reverend John Badders, dean of the Iona School in the Diocese of West Texas, who flew an "airplane we are building as we fly it," thank you for your humble nature that all priests should learn and imitate.

Thank you to the Church of the Advent in Alice, Texas, and the Reverend Tom Turner, who kindly took me in as a seminarian, taught me what it means to preach to a congregation, and was kind enough to welcome me when I visited.

To Saint Philip's Church in Beeville, Texas, who nurtured my sense of calling, shared me with the parish in Alice, and walked with me on my discernment and eventual call to the priesthood, thank you. No one could have had a better and more dedicated sending parish than Saint Philip's, and all of you will always hold a special place in my heart.

Thank you to Kenneth Bethune, Lindsay Horton, Nick Ottensman, and Courtney and Jarrad Williams who read a few of these sermons and helped me excise a few sermons from this collection that I had doubts about. They were willing to look over the manuscript, give feedback, and pointedly say if they had no idea as regular lay people what something meant. It was help that was most invaluable indeed!

Thank you to the Reverend Armando Alejandro, my dear friend from the Roman Catholic Church, who journeyed with me in a different faith tradition and in a different seminary but nonetheless provided encouragement and prayers along the way. May our Lady of Walsingham keep you in her prayers.

To the Reverend Canon Carl Turner, Rector of Saint Thomas Church Fifth Avenue, New York City, thank you. You were willing from afar to read and comment but also offer prayers at Saint Thomas for my colleagues and me as we approached ordination.

Thank you to my mother, Linda, who probably heard each of these sermons before anyone else and always listened (and sometimes interrupted) as I practiced delivering them.

To the Right Reverend David Reed, X Bishop of the Diocese of West Texas, thank you for your vision for beginning the Iona Program and School in our Diocese and for your leadership and guidance as not only a bishop but also a friend and pastor.

To Drs. Randall Bradley and Terry York of Baylor University, Waco, Texas, who were mentors and professors during my undergraduate and graduate years, thank you. Together, they read almost every word in this small volume. They have changed their roles, transforming from professors and mentors to friends. Even when I struggled with some of these sermons, they provided both the needed humor and grace to continue in this process.

Finally, I must thank the Reverend Brian Tarver, now Rector of Saint David's Church in San Antonio, Texas. Father Brian came to Saint Philip's just as I was beginning the seminary process and at our first meeting between rector and organist said, "So, I understand I'm losing my organist in three years." He may have lost his organist, but I have gained a most valued friend and colleague. From listening to the joys and woes of life during our time serving together to reading every sermon I wrote and preached, to encouraging me to tell more stories, giving me the opportunities to teach and trusting me with stepping into the pulpit when he was away from time to time, no one could have asked for a more supportive pastor and friend. Father Brian is someone who continues to read, mark, learn, and inwardly digest the Holy Scriptures. He is a gifted homilist and preacher whose dedication and art he puts into his teaching and each of the sermons he crafts. I am not certain he even knows he was sharing that gift with me. So to my dear friend Brian, I humbly dedicate this book.

CPSIA information can be obtained
at www.ICGtesting.com
Printed in the USA
BVHW090015111121
621204BV00011B/909